121 DAYS

www.mascotbooks.com

121 Days: The Corbin Raymond Story of Fighting for Life and Surviving a Traumatic Brain Injury

I have tried to recreate events, locales, and conversations from my memories of them. In order to maintain their anonymity in some instances I have changed the names of individuals and places. I may have changed some identifying characteristics and details such as physical properties, occupations, and places of residence.

For more information, please contact:
Mascot Books
620 Herndon Parkway #320
Herndon, VA 20170
info@mascotbooks.com

Library of Congress Control Number: 2020913964

CPSIA Code: PRV1020A
ISBN-13: 978-1-64543-272-2

Printed in the United States

For my children: Corbin, Grace, Cohen, and Grayson. You guys are my whole world. No more trips to the emergency room, please.

P.S. You're all my favorite.

121 DAYS

THE CORBIN RAYMOND STORY
OF FIGHTING FOR LIFE AND SURVIVING A TRAUMATIC BRAIN INJURY

SADIE RAYMOND
WITH TODD CIVIN

FOREWORD

It's almost hard to describe the sheer admiration I feel for Sadie and how she handled the horrific situation she was faced with. I found it remarkable to watch her as she dealt with the tragic events and the very real possibility of losing her son. It was as if she donned a giant, powerful shield—a shield that would protect her family, not allowing anything bad to happen—refusing to take "no" for an answer. It was amazing to see the strength and emotional steadiness that she showed EVERY SINGLE DAY. I often wondered how she could hold it together for so many hours, day after day, while many of us around her were falling apart. She was an incredible advocate for Corbin, questioning and pushing for answers, demanding nothing but the very best. She was the ultimate Mama Bear!

But the one thing I remember most, that struck me to my core, was when the surgeon came out and said there was nothing more that could be done. The doctor said that Corbin's injuries were "catastrophic" and to gather his family to say goodbye. But Sadie didn't burst out crying . . . she didn't fall apart. She said, "Is he still alive?" And the doctor said yes. Then Sadie said, "As long as his heart is beating, and I can hold his hand and tell him I love him every day, that's good enough for me."

So, every tiny bit of progress Corbin made—even as simple as moving his finger—brought tremendous happiness and celebration. Sadie would say, "I'll take it!" To see his incredible progress, and to witness Sadie throughout this whole ordeal, was nothing short of miraculous.

Brenda Baron
Grayson's Nana
Local Interior Designer

1

A MEMORABLE
INDEPENDENCE DAY

For the first dozen years of my married life, we celebrated the Fourth of July with a much-anticipated party at our Boscawen, New Hampshire, home. It had become a huge part of the family tradition that America's independence would be acknowledged in the Raymond's backyard complete with family, friends, and more of the kids' friends than we'd ever stop to count. We looked forward to it and we wouldn't want it any other way. From just before noontime until the wee hours, we'd enjoy burgers, dogs, watermelon, countless homemade side dishes, and s'mores, splash loudly in the pool and ingest a healthy dose of calories, laughter, and libations. The daylong celebration would be capped off with our very own New Hampshire legal, homegrown firework display in the sky above our home.

For most of those celebrations, Jeff and I played gracious hosts to anyone who happened to show up and, for years on end, the day was filled with joyous memories. After Jeff and I divorced, the tradition continued but instead with my boyfriend, Steve, taking over as the acting grill master and the male head of the household. The Fourth of July, in the year 2018, became as unforgettable as those that preceded it, but for a completely different reason and one we will remember much longer than any of America's prior birthday celebrations. Unfortunately, the memories that will be forever etched in Raymond family lore were not those of sparklers, fireworks, and burgers on the grill. Instead, we were left with the life-altering sights, sounds, and recollections of horror, heartache, and tragedy.

As that fateful morning began, I opened one eye and then the other, as the sun snuck through a slight crack that I had left between the bottom of the shade and the windowsill. I contemplated rolling over, putting the pillow back over my head, and falling back to sleep. However, I knew that I had a full day of work ahead of me. That year, the Fourth wouldn't consist of celebrating with friends, flipping burgers, or drinking from red Solo cups filled with beer. Instead, I'd be bartending at CC Tomatoes, a local restaurant in Concord where I worked part-time. It was far from glamourous, but it paid the bills and unfortunately, life was in a place where that was becoming necessary.

I let out a cat-like stretch, slithered from beneath the sheets, and began the holiday as a forty-year-old, single mother of four children. My life was certainly not at its peak as I peered at my tired-looking reflection in the full-length mirror that hung from my bedroom wall. Jeff and I had parted ways about four-and-a-half years ago, and I found myself in a failing relationship yet again. Only this time, it was with the father of my two-year-old son, Grayson. My soon to be halted relationship with Steve was challenging right from the beginning.

Like the little girl with the curl, we were either really good or really bad with very little in between. We were smoking hot or freezing cold, but never lukewarm. We shared very few mutual friends, and during any free time we would usually stay home with the kids and ignore each other. Or, we would go to his mother's house in Nashua to visit. He was always on the verge of moving out and, quite fittingly, he scheduled two days after the Fourth to officially pack his bags and finally provide us both with our independence.

My life hardly screamed of independence at the time, and instead, it seemed to constantly shout back at me, "What the hell did you do to deserve this?" Without my four incredible children, who I love more than life itself, and an extremely supportive family and circle of friends, I'm not quite sure how I survived each day. I wasn't certain what life would hand me next, leaving me questioning how I ever managed to get in this position and what I needed to do to straighten out my family's slightly runaway course. As a parent, whether with a partner or not, it was my obligation to ensure that my family did not suffer one bit as a result of my ill-advised decision-making skills.

I began bartending several nights a week to create some much-needed cash flow for my suddenly single-income family. I chose the evening bartending schedule so that I could be home during the day with Grayson, while Corbin, Grace, and Cohen attended school. Though I had hoped to spend at least part of the day with the kids to celebrate America's 242nd birthday, Corbin and Grace made plans with their friends, Jeff offered to take care of Cohen, and Steve took Grayson to his family's house. So, I gave in to working a double shift hoping to earn some extra tips courtesy of any patrons who may have chosen to spend their Independence Day sitting at a bar.

Corbin, who was sixteen going on "man of the house," made plans to celebrate his own sense of independence and was pumped to meet up with his cousin, Tanna, and a few buddies to tube down the Merrimack River that afternoon. When he asked me if he could go, I was very hesitant. The other boys wanted to tube partway down the river, camp out on the beach overnight, and float the rest of the way down the gentle rapids the next morning. None of the kids had their driver's licenses for even a year, and the thought of them being alone on the river reminded me a bit too much of what I was likely doing at the same age.

I have always been a little overprotective of my children, so I argued with myself whether or not to let him hang with his buddies for the day. Corbin was scheduled to work that night so he would only be on the river a few hours and not overnight like the other boys. Much against my better judgment, I reluctantly agreed.

I had to be at work by 10 a.m. to prep for the lunchtime crowd, so I did my best to make myself presentable to face the long day ahead. I made it downstairs and searched the kitchen counter for my always elusive car keys. It seemed like nothing was easy for me these days and even starting the SUV involved a quick game of hide-and-seek. I heard Corbin shut the shower water off and step onto the bathroom tile. I tapped on the bathroom door to go over his plans for the day and to request a comforting promise that he would be careful and behave. No mother feels right without instructing their child to be careful (as if it does any good whatsoever).

A typical teenage boy and likely wrapped in a towel, he responded through the bathroom door and gave me a half-hearted

"Goodbye, Mom" without actually seeing me. Not entirely comfortable with my decision to let him go, I mothered him a bit more and told him to text me when he left the house to recap his game plan for the day. He begrudgingly agreed and advised me that Grace was still in bed sleeping.

The bar opened at 11 a.m., and I was expecting it to be rather slow, knowing how beautiful the weather was supposed to be. I stocked the bar with a few buckets of ice, cut up some lemons and limes, gave the bar area a quick vacuum, and waited for at least one patron to provide me with someone to chat with. My first and, what would be, my only customer of the day, came in shortly after opening and ordered a sandwich for lunch. I recognized him from years prior when our boys were little, so we started reminiscing about their T-ball days. We chatted about how quickly they grow up and ironically, how scary it can be when those same little toddlers become old enough to get their driver's licenses.

The unfamiliar tone of my new cell phone interrupted our conversation. I had just gotten it a few days earlier so I hadn't transferred all my contacts over yet. Unable to recognize the number of the incoming call and not wanting to be rude, I decided not to answer, figuring that they would call me back if we really needed to connect. In an eerie case of foreshadowing, my customer continued the conversation and shared a story about how his son was recently in a fender bender on the highway. He told me that it was one of those situations where traffic suddenly came to a halt and unable to react quickly enough, his son rear-ended the car in front of him.

Luckily, no one was injured, and he chalked it up to the inexperience of his son behind the wheel, perhaps tailgating a bit, but hopefully not engaging in teens' favorite current pastime, texting.

He wasn't quite finished sharing the story when I heard the ping of my phone advising me that I had a text. Steve's number was one that I certainly recognized even without having his contact added to my phone. His text ordered me to call him immediately. "It's an EMERGENCY," he texted, likely knowing that without such detail and the capital letters, I would ignore him and not hurry to return his call.

All I could think was that something had happened to Grayson. They were going to be at his sister's pool for the day. I immediately got a huge lump in my throat and assumed the worst. I excused myself from my customer and called Steve in a near panic. He let me know that Grayson was fine, but he had received a call from my sister-in-law, Kim. She told him that my nephew, Tanna, had been in an accident and was reportedly trapped inside the vehicle. Corbin and Tanna are first cousins and have been nearly inseparable since he moved up from Florida in 2014.

I wasn't sure why she chose to notify me first, but I assumed that I must be closest to the accident so was the first one called. An instant later it hit me that Tanna was supposed to be with Corbin on the tubing trip. The decibel level of my voice increased as I peppered Steve with questions in rapid succession as soon as I realized that the boys were likely together. "Where are they? Where is the accident? Was Corbin with him?" Steve tried to get me to calm down, while letting me know the road the accident was on.

I hung up the phone without saying goodbye, much like many calls Steve and I had over the past several months. I quivered uncontrollably, not sure what to do first. In a state of mild hysteria, I began asking myself a new series of questions under my breath. "Should I go to the hospital? Should I head to the road where the accident was? Oh my God! Was Corbin in that car?" The speed of my breaths heightened, and I knew I had to gain control of my emotions before I boiled over. I ran over to my coworker, told her about the call, asked her to serve the sandwich to my now abandoned customer, and then bolted out the door.

I flew across the parking lot, my feet hardly touching the pavement, and threw my SUV into drive while simultaneously jamming the gas pedal to the floor. I immediately dialed my mother while on the way to see if she had perhaps heard what happened. Mom answered the phone, sounding almost as frantic as I was. She told me that Kim had called her as well. She had been notified about the accident via her Life360 app and asked Mom to get to the hospital as soon as possible because she and my brother Chris were on their boat for the day. They were coincidentally boating on the same river that the boys were headed for, and she didn't know how fast they could get to shore and the accident scene.

My mother had no details about Corbin and that helped me in making my decision to head straight to the scene of the accident. As I sped down Fishersville Road with absolutely no concern of the speed limit or oncoming vehicles, I glanced down at the dash and saw an all too familiar sight. The bright orange light on my gas gauge greeted me and indicated that I had once again ignored its warning the night before. "God, damn it! Not now!" I screamed to myself, out loud, for only me to hear.

I had worked late, and I noticed the low fuel light was on but true to habit I procrastinated. With so much going on in my daily life, I think I do a pretty good job keeping up with everything thrown at me in real-time, with little delay. However, the one area that I fail miserably in, over and over again, is filling my gas tank despite the warnings.

Lo and behold, it would soon bite me in the ass. When I needed it most, I was running on fumes and despite the reality of the situation, I was still debating whether or not I had enough fumes to get to the accident scene. My mind played tug of war with itself, as it so often does when I'm in this position. Do I stop at the next station and get a bit of gas so as not to delay myself? Or, do I pray for an act of God and try to make it to the scene of the accident?

What if I run out on the way there and find myself stranded? I knew the right answer to my litany of questions, but as I've often done throughout my life, I made the wrong decision and I decided to risk it. I had to know that Corbin was fine and, Lord willing, no lack of fuel was going to delay me from getting there.

I sped toward River Road and dialed up Grace over and over with no answer. As soon as it went to voice mail, I'd hang up and neurotically press redial in hopes of a different result. I just wanted her to tell me that somehow Corbin had been delayed and hadn't left the house yet. Corbin hadn't texted me to tell me that he was leaving, as I had instructed him to, so he must still be there or so I desperately wanted to believe. I gave up on connecting with Grace and began calling Corbin's phone with the same maniacal repetition as I had his sister's. Ring, voice mail, hang up, dial. Ring, voice mail, hang up, dial.

During my incessant dialing fit, I hadn't even noticed that I had reached River Road. The knot in my stomach seemed to climb up into my throat as I swerved recklessly onto River Road without any thought of flipping on my directional light. *What am I going to see?* Even if Corbin miraculously wasn't involved in the accident, my nephew was reportedly trapped in the vehicle. I knew the scene that awaited me was not something anyone looks forward to witnessing. The thoughts whipped through my mind one after another without even a second of delay in between.

I felt like I had been driving for much longer than expected as I passed one of the popular spots where people put their tubes into the river or go swimming. Groups of kids were laughing and screaming with excitement as I drove by in a completely opposite mindset. No one looked as though they had just witnessed a horrific accident like I anticipated seeing. Again, my mind and inner voice took control of the dialogue.

Maybe this was all a bad dream or was blown out of proportion. Maybe this was a blessing to get me out of working on a day that I really didn't want to be there anyhow. I was going to come upon a slight fender bender, exchange insurance papers, and head back home to spend the day barbecuing after all. I continued to feel like this was the longest drive of my life. I had been on River Road hundreds of times, and it never felt this long. Each minute that passed gave me a bit more hope with the belief that I should have come across the wreck by now.

Suddenly, the tar road seemed to turn to dirt, and all I could see ahead were flashing lights. I drove as close as I could before a wall of emergency vehicles prevented me from getting any closer. I threw my SUV into park and jumped out with no concern of closing the door behind me. As I ran frantically toward the lights, I stumbled upon an odd thought. I was confused by the fact that the road was dirt when, to my knowledge, it was a completely paved road.

The experience was so surreal. If I hadn't felt a burst of hot summer air hit my face, I may have been able to convince myself that this was a weird, horrible dream. Instead, I'd soon realize that it was the beginning of our real-life nightmare. After a few more steps, I realized that the vehicle had torn through people's yards and woods covering the unrecognizable road in a furrow of dirt, burying the pavement underneath.

A police officer grabbed me by the upper left arm as I tried to maneuver my way through the sea of rescue workers. I tried to wrestle my way by him like a football player trying to break a tackle. His attempt to slow me down and stop me was successful. I found myself momentarily speechless, standing ankle-deep in dirt. I came face-to-face with a white car on its side hurled up against a tree. Tears welled up in my eyes as my hand came to my mouth.

The vehicle had no roof, and its entire white interior was saturated with blood. I was briefly relieved upon witnessing the sight of the car. "I don't even know that car. None of Corbin's friends drive a convertible." Though a momentary reprieve, I remember feeling a slight sense of relief, my mind constantly searching for any reason to excuse this as someone else's tragedy and not mine. Sure, I'd feel horrible that "their Corbin" had been injured in a horrible crash, but my Corbin was joyfully tubing down the river on the Fourth as planned.

I snapped back to reality, pulled my arm away from the officer, and said, "I think my nephew was in this accident." The officer calmly asked me his name and then confirmed that Tanna was indeed a victim in the accident. He told me that he had been removed from the vehicle and was being tended to in the ambulance that was parked to the right of the accident scene.

Though frantic, I reluctantly asked if Corbin was also in the vehicle. I felt the police officer hesitate slightly. Though his pause was negligible, it was long enough that I noted his delay. I knew his answer before he told me. Corbin was not only in the vehicle but he had also suffered the most severe injuries. Another ambulance had already rushed him to the hospital.

Again, I tried to understand why the medical team seemed to be so calmly working on my nephew at the scene of the accident, while Corbin had been whisked away in an ambulance. How could two injuries in the same demolished vehicle be so different?

I beckoned the officer to tell me the extent of Corbin's injuries or to provide me with any calming information at all. I peppered him with questions, which were all just variations of the question, "Is my son okay?" All the officer would say was that Corbin was alive when he left in the ambulance. There was little or no comfort in those hollow words and, though I knew he was simply doing his job, I didn't care.

I needed to find out, and find out now, whether or not my son was okay.

I hushed the officer mid-sentence, reversed field, and ran just as quickly back to my SUV. The door was still open, and it was covered with a thick layer of dust that had settled on the hood, windshield, and the front seat. With the gas gauge still gasping for breath, I threw the vehicle into reverse and unintentionally spun my tires as I headed for the hospital.

2

NAKED AND LIFELESS

s I careened down River Road and past the kids still frolicking unknowingly in the river, I tried to convince myself that it wasn't going to be that bad. My life has been far from perfect, but I couldn't comprehend that anything catastrophic could ever happen to my child. Things like this happened to other families, but not to mine.

About two minutes down the road, the gas light caught the corner of my eye. Even in my current level of insanity, I was of sound enough mind to know that it was not possible for me to make it to the hospital without gas. I stopped at the station right next to my work, fumbled for my debit card, which of course, was hiding behind several rarely used cards in my wallet and began pumping. It should have come as no surprise that the pump was uncooperative and flashed zeroes indefinitely, until it finally granted me the privilege of pumping some gas into my tank.

Another shocker, to absolutely no one, was the fact that I

had decided to only pump enough fuel to get me to the hospital instead of filling up since that was how I usually rolled. As I started pumping, my cousin's daughter, Autumn, ran up to wish me a happy Fourth and give me a hug. She was dressed in clothes that indicated she was ready for the beach and had stopped for some last-minute munchies.

I could barely speak as she grabbed me lovingly. I think I got out a jumbled phrase intended to be, "Corbin's been in an accident." My hands were shaking holding the gas pump. As soon as the numbers on the pump hit three dollars, I knew I had enough to get me there. Shocked by my announcement, she offered to drive me to the hospital but I politely, or perhaps even impolitely, refused. I just wanted to get in my car and get there as fast as I could. As loving as she is, she immediately halted her plans of heading to the beach and agreed to follow me to the hospital.

I involuntarily spun my tires again as I exited the gas station, without any concern of whether or not there were other patrons in my path. This was all about me at the moment, with no concern for the health and well-being of anyone but Corbin. I started to make phone calls, first to my mom. I confirmed to her that Corbin was in the accident, but she was already preemptively waiting at the hospital anyhow. To that point, neither of the boys' ambulances had arrived and she couldn't find out anything about their condition. Though knowing Mom, she had most definitely interrogated the ER staff to pick up any morsel of information they may have dropped.

I banged out the numbers to Corbin's father a half-dozen times without being able to reach him. Again, dial, voice mail, dial, voice mail before succumbing and leaving a garbled message that Corbin was in an accident and I had no idea about his condition. This wasn't the kind of message you want to leave on voice mail, but what was I to do? I then called Grace and told her that she needed to get a ride to the hospital immediately. I needed the family to be together so that we could all assure each other that everything was going to be okay.

As I was driving, I noticed a truck a few vehicles back from me weaving in and out of traffic, swerving and flashing its lights. It was my brother, Chris, Tanna's dad, also rushing to the hospital not knowing the condition of his son or Corbin. We arrived at the ER within seconds of each other and found my mother and my nephew's mother at the check-in desk. They still hadn't received any information on the boys' condition.

By the time I ran in with my brother and cousin, they told us they would escort all of us inside to a private family waiting room and a doctor would be in to speak with us. That was nice of them but didn't sound like the type of over-considerate service we were hoping to receive. We grouped together for a moment as a family, tried to calm ourselves down, and walked at a quick pace, together toward the waiting room.

As we walked through the ER halls toward the waiting area, I noticed some kids Corbin went to school with, standing up and staring at us. They each had a look of absolute concern and fear on their collective faces. In the cell phone era that we live in, grapevine communication spreads like wildfire and several of Corbin's friends had ascended on the hospital and arrived even before we did. All I could wonder was whether they knew something, that we didn't.

Once we were in the private waiting room, other family members started to show up. We sat there for what seemed like hours, not knowing anything more than the information of what our runaway minds would provide us with. It was difficult not to envision the worst, but even in the infancy of this ordeal, I remained positive. I actually shocked myself as one is never certain how they will respond in times of tragedy. I assumed I would be frantic and out of control, thinking nothing but the worst. However, I was surprisingly confident that everything was going to be okay. I believe that is referred to as denial, but, nonetheless, I was relatively in control.

Our group paced around the room, occasionally sitting, randomly speaking. We also engaged in long periods of silence where no one spoke, but remained deep in thought, sorting through the details in our minds. A nurse, the first staff member to break the family silence, entered the room and asked which one of us was Corbin's mother. I jumped up and raised my hand upon hearing her say that she would take me to see Corbin now. *Thank goodness. That means he's fine,* was all I could think as I bolted through the waiting room doors and into the hallway.

She then locked elbows with me with one arm and wrapped her other arm around my back to support me. It was as if she expected me to fall down upon seeing Corbin. Chris joined us and asked if he could come with me, so I wasn't alone. My response would have been irrelevant as Chris had decided to accompany me, regardless of my answer. I was still stuck on why I was being held that way, and said, "Of course, you can come."

The next sight was one that will never escape my mind for as long as I live. The nurse walked us into this big open area that had no doors. She pulled up a chair and told me to sit down. Corbin was on a table in the center of the room. He was naked. Lifeless. Corbin was covered, and I mean covered, from head to toe, with blood. He had wires going into his body in more places than I could comprehend, hooked up to fluids, with bags of blood entering his body, and all kinds of machines doing everything they could to keep him alive.

There were about thirty doctors, nurses, and specialists working on him in symphony, like the machines, all with a sense of purpose. They wasted no time, working in unison on the naked body of my son. The only time I saw any of them stop, for even a second, was when several of them would peer over their surgical masks in my direction with what I interpreted as a sad, fearful expression that was making me extremely uncomfortable. No one spoke. No one explained what was going on. They spoke to each other in medical lingo, passing around tools like a group of auto mechanics fixing a finely tuned vehicle as I sat and watched like the sole member of the audience watching a tragedy.

I was an observer, sitting and experiencing the worse nightmare I could ever imagine. It honestly felt like a night terror, where you wake up sick to your stomach in a cold sweat and wonder what your mind had just conjured up. I couldn't understand why I was there. Why would they do this? Why would they want me to watch my son in such a state of disrepair?

I felt like I was in a torture chamber in a low budget horror movie. My brother stood behind me rubbing my shoulders, quietly assuring me that everything was going to be okay, when clearly it was not. He assured me that we were going to get through this. That's when I went numb. It all stopped feeling real.

While we were seemingly watching Corbin dying together, Chris asked a nurse if she knew the condition of Tanna. It wasn't lost on me that here was Chris sitting with me, consoling me, without knowing the extent of his own son's injuries. The nurse explained that Tanna was in a room right behind us, and I urged

Chris to go. "Go see Tanna," I insisted. I assured him that I was okay and that he had to go see his son.

A minute later, the same nurse grabbed my arm, helped me to my feet, and led me back to the waiting room. Again, with no explanation except to say that a doctor would be in shortly. I honestly felt like I was in heaven, being brought from one section to another, looking down on my life below with none of the angels considerate enough to describe what I was seeing. It was in a word "eerie." I couldn't even begin to explain to my family what I had just seen. I was not able to muster so much as a syllable as I sat there expressionless with tears flowing down my face, and onto my chin, before dropping off into a quickly growing puddle onto the floor below.

Upon reentering the waiting room, I noticed that Grace, her stepsister, Mari, and Steve had arrived. Though Steve and I never married, we had lived as a family for six years. So, even though Mari wasn't my children's stepsister, they considered her as such. I tried to call Jeff several more times so that the entire family, such that it is, could be present to support each other. Though we had become a rather dysfunctional family unit, we needed to put all the BS aside and support Corbin and each other. I left Jeff an extremely broken message attempting to tell him that Corbin wasn't in good condition and that he needed to get to the hospital right away.

I can only imagine what the message sounded like from his side of the phone as I alternated sniffles and snorts surrounded by an occasional unintelligible word. Grace thought that perhaps Jeff was up north with his new wife's family. So, she tried to reach out to them, while I tried his mother to see if she could locate him.

Finally, a doctor interrupted our long wait and entered the

room with the first of what would be many explanations of Corbin's current condition. She didn't sugarcoat anything, but she told it like it is, business-like and professional, but not cold. We listened intently as she explained that Corbin had suffered many injuries throughout his entire body, but most severe was the head trauma.

She said they had been working on getting him stable enough to bring him to the operating room. She advised us that he had a punctured lung, he had lost a lot of blood, and that they were sure they were going to find much more damage when they were finally able to open him up. The catalog of issues continued like a grocery list created from a medical journal as she told us that his brain was swelling, and they may need to remove part of his skull.

With each addition to the endless inventory of injuries, I felt my stomach do another flip, but I knew I needed to keep it together. The doctor then asked if they had my permission to remove part of his skull and continue. I reflexed without thought and said, "Of course. Do whatever you have to do to save him." It was a very fast interaction. At the same time, it alarmed me a bit to consider that any mother would give a different answer. For me, there was no other option. Even in these early stages, I had decided that Corbin's survival was the only option.

The doctor hustled out and a nurse escorted us to the waiting room outside of the ER. Once we got there, family members continued to arrive. All of them greeted us with long hugs, tears, and an endless stream of repeat questions that we didn't have solid answers for. We were obviously still in the early stages of wait and see mode. There was still no word from Jeff, who also had Corbin's younger brother, Cohen, with him.

As we were going upstairs, Corbin's cousin Paul arrived. Paul has been in the medical field in one way or another for as long as I can remember. He hugged me and then very calmly asked me what I knew about Corbin's condition. I explained what the surgeon told me. Paul took immediate control of the situation having a fairly thorough understanding of how the industry works.

He asked if I felt satisfied with what I knew about Corbin's condition. I thought about it for a second and said no not really. I felt the doctor told me very little considering the life of my oldest son was hanging in delicate balance. Had he broken his ankle or skinned his knee, I would have been okay with her explanation, but not when my son's life is in jeopardy. Paul put his arm around my shoulders comfortingly as we walked back to the ER and approached another surgeon who had worked on Corbin. Paul asked if he could join us and answer some of our many questions.

Though I was only a few feet away from him and Paul, I could see his lips moving but couldn't hear what he was saying. Paul asked him some questions in medical terms, but all I deciphered from the conversation was how bad the damage to Corbin's head was. Paul asked the surgeon if he thought Corbin should be transferred to a Level 1 trauma center if he survived surgery. The surgeon's answer was an abrupt no. He believed that this hospital was well enough equipped to treat Corbin. The conversation ended at that point, and we headed back upstairs.

I asked Paul why he discussed transferring him, and he explained that a Level 1 trauma hospital like Boston Children's Hospital is much better equipped to handle this kind of trauma. He explained that despite the surgeon's firm response, we have that option and we can demand that. I had never heard of this and would not have known, had Paul not been acutely aware of how things function in this world. No call to insurance was needed, simply the family advocating for the patient and taking control of their care. I knew at that point that Paul was there for a reason and would ultimately be invaluable throughout this whole ordeal.

By the time we got back upstairs, my phone was ringing. At last, it was Jeff. He sounded extremely distraught, as can be expected, after listening to my countless frantic messages. By the time I finished explaining how bad the accident was and advising him of Corbin's condition, he was screaming; not at me, but simply in a fit of uncontrolled panic. He said they were on their way and would try to get there as soon as possible. They had been on a boat in the lake and just got back into the service area that was still some distance away from the hospital.

In the meantime, our crowd had grown to about twenty family members and friends, waiting for any word emanating from the operating room. We all talked as calmly as we could and assured each other that everything was going to be okay. I'm not sure that any of us really believed it, but that's the approach we had all chosen and there was strength in numbers.

Jeff's sister, Christine, said, "He just has to survive it and then we'll deal with the rest." To that point, I hadn't even considered that option. I was simply thinking that he was going to end up perfectly fine once he survived and healed and hadn't even realized that he may be severely impacted once he is out of immediate danger. I found myself reasoning and bargaining for any possible chance of him being okay.

I refused to believe that he wasn't going to make it. I was simply not going to let him go and there was no way in my head that I was going to allow anything but a full recovery to occur. I knew darn well that I wasn't in control, but I was going to wrestle whoever I had to in order to ensure Corbin's survival.

After several hours of waiting, a nurse exited the operating room and told us that they would be wheeling Corbin to ICU recovery. For a split second, we got excited at the thought of seeing him. Though I knew I was fantasizing, I envisioned him getting wheeled by with his head bandaged and giving me a thumbs up and a wink as he wheeled by, like he had sustained an ankle injury on a football field.

The nurse snapped me back to reality when she advised us that they would really like us to stay in the waiting room. Corbin was still not in great shape and they didn't want everyone to see him. I looked right at Christine and instead of being upset as one might think, I screamed, "HE'S ALIVE!"

As she had advised us earlier, she said, "Yes, and we'll deal with the rest."

3

BECOMING CORBIN'S ADVOCATE

t was a huge feeling of relief. He made it. He survived the surgery! I hadn't even considered that this was simply the first of many surgeries. In my naïve mind, I thought that he made it through surgery and now we just needed to be patient. I knew Corbin was a tough kid. I believed that if he made it through surgery, the rest was going to follow in the same way.

I never believed it was going to be easy, but somehow, I convinced myself that before it was in the hands of Corbin and the doctors. After the surgery, his recovery belonged to Corbin and me.

A few minutes later, the female surgeon and a gentleman came out to speak to us. As she was explaining what they did in surgery, my attention was suddenly snatched away when I saw the elevator doors slowly open. I immediately spotted Jeff, his wife Angela, their daughter, and Cohen rushing through the doors and into the hallway before the doors even opened completely. I asked the doctor to wait just a moment so Corbin's dad could hear the long list of procedures that the medical team had performed to keep our son alive.

She stopped momentarily, but everyone rampaged her with a series of questions resembling a group of reporters with their microphones stuffed under the chin of a politician. "Doctor, is he going to be okay?" "Will he be the same?" As Jeff stepped into the room, the other man, who was introduced to us as a neurologist, left all bedside manner in the operating room and advised us tersely that Corbin's injuries were so catastrophic that he would not survive. His brain was showing no signs of response or activity.

The entire room heard his harrowing statement and in unison lost control. For some reason, I didn't react in quite the same way. Though the neurologist was essentially pulling the white sheet over Corbin's face, I failed to comprehend what he had just stated. I was caught off guard and perhaps it took me a while longer to process what he had told us. I sat there and noted everyone's response for several seconds.

I also noticed that the doctor appeared agitated with the blatant disregard that the neurologist exhibited. Was it his frank and rather matter of fact presentation, or did she think that he had made his determination too early in the process? Something was very off to me. I watched everyone crying and hugging each other. I heard my mother sobbing uncontrollably, and witnessed Jeff physically try to put himself through a wall screaming the word "NO" at the top of his lungs.

All I could focus on was the thought that he was still alive. Maybe, it was a severe case of denial, but I didn't move a stitch. I didn't freak out. I just kept telling myself, *he is alive and nothing else matters at this moment.* Cohen and Grace both rushed to me, each crying on a different shoulder.

I felt robotic and I remember hearing my mother order the doctor to get me something to calm my nerves because I was clearly in a state of shock. She was likely right. I wasn't speaking, and I never left my chair. Everyone kept coming up and trying to console me, but I couldn't focus or say anything to them. I looked up slowly and made eye contact with the surgeon. Still not a peep escaped my mouth.

She came over, knelt down beside me, and put her hand on my arm. She explained to me what they did to Corbin in the OR. He had his spleen removed, his bowels repaired, a large blood transfusion, a monitor drilled into his skull to track the pressure from his swelling brain, and drains put in his lungs. After that laundry list of surgical procedures performed on my son, she started to explain the damage to his brain and that his pupils didn't react to light. I sat and listened, speechless.

When she finished, the first words finally escaped from my lips. I said, "But he's still alive right now, right?" She began to respond and said, "yes but—" I immediately interrupted her before she could say the next syllable. I said, "Then I want him transferred to Boston Children's Hospital."

She stated a few things to try and dissuade me from my decision. "Well, he has to be stable enough to travel. We don't even know if they have rooms available. We don't even know if they will take him." I heard none of it, or more specifically, I refused to accept no for an answer. "Then let's find out," I said. I had always heard people say that you need to be an advocate for yourself in these situations. Since Corbin clearly was in no condition to do that on his own, I was going to become his very capable stand-in.

From this point on, the hospital was going to make suggestions and I was going to make decisions, not vice versa. It is my son whose life is in peril and though I believed the staff was very capable, to them a potential casualty is just a statistic and not their son. I was in the driver's seat moving forward, and I was belted in and ready for a long ride.

I told her that I wanted to see him as soon as possible. She agreed immediately, much like a PFC who was taking orders from a drill sergeant before disappearing. I was determined to get him out of there as fast as possible and on a Life Flight to Boston Children's Hospital or any facility that was better suited to produce a positive result.

About fifteen minutes passed and the neurologist returned. He did an about-face and informed us that he was witnessing a few good signs. I'm not sure if anything had actually changed or if the surgeon had reprimanded him behind closed doors. He told us that one of Corbin's pupils was responding slightly to light now. Not a huge triumph, but it was something. A small victory on the way to what we hoped would become an endless string of small victories.

They took Jeff and me back to see him. Though Jeff and I had stopped being a couple, some time before, our son's life was hanging in the balance. Suddenly, all of our differences were temporarily behind us, and we were working together for the good of our son. We walked into the room together and simultaneously laid our eyes on Corbin. He was a mess. There is no other way to describe him. Almost like a Picasso painting, with his nose where his forehead should have been and his mouth about three times the size of the norm.

I felt so relieved to hold his warm hand and see his chest move as he took a breath, that I didn't process how absolutely mashed up my son looked. One nurse was putting little stitches in on the lacerations on his face, and another nurse had a small piece of folded tape that she was using to remove shards of glass from his shoulder. I immediately wondered, why would they be concerned about shards of glass if he wasn't going to survive? I interpreted this as a positive sign.

Jeff and I began talking to him to assure him that he was not alone. We had no idea if Corbin could hear us or whether he even possessed the capability to understand. But we weren't leaving anything to chance. We told him we were there with him and that we loved him. We assured him that he was going to be okay.

Not long after, Corbin began to crash, and they ushered us out of the room so they could tend to him. I persisted about getting him on a flight to Boston, and within an hour a helicopter was there prepared to depart to BCH. I guess they knew that Mama Bear meant business. They let us back in to be with him until the flight crew was ready to wheel him away. Even moving him from the bed to the stretcher made his vital signs go haywire, and we were whisked out of the room again.

We were able to kiss him goodbye before they wheeled him to the helicopter. The flight crew told us not to rush to Boston. We would not be able to see him right away anyhow, and we should plan on being down there for quite a while. They encouraged us to go home, pack a bag, and get something to eat.

Don't rush? Eat? I fully understand why they told us these things, but who in their right mind would not immediately rush to Boston? How would I ever be able to eat at a time like this? Somehow sitting down to a nice casual meal while my son was clinging to life didn't seem like a very likely scenario. My mind was focused solely on getting back to Corbin's side as fast as I could, to continue to be his advocate, and to forever remain his mother.

Jeff and I went back to the waiting room and attempted to calmly explain it all to our families. Just about everyone insisted on going to Boston with us, which we could understand, but we asked them to refrain from coming down so soon. There would be time for that. Corbin was by no means out of the woods and was, more accurately, deep in the middle of the forest. He was so unstable, we were just praying he survived the flight.

At that point, I began living my life, not day by day, but hour by hour. I knew I could handle this if I took it in small increments. I couldn't think too far ahead because I didn't even know if he was going to survive. I used my best coping mechanism, and I lived in the right here, right now. First, we made it through the surgery. Next, we need to make it through the flight. We can't get too far ahead of ourselves. One moment, one event at a time, one obstacle overcome before we can even consider what lies ahead.

Steve drove me home, and we both threw together a bag of essentials. There wasn't much talking. We had gotten to the point in our relationship that we didn't talk that much anyhow. Though, under these circumstances, the silence was the result of being deep in thought and processing all that needed to be processed. For some morbid reason, we decided to drive by the accident scene on our way to Boston. We needed to witness the accident scene now that all the chaos had dissipated. When we came around the corner, we saw the tree that ultimately stopped the car.

Not surprisingly, we saw Jeff standing on the side of the road doing exactly the same thing we were. He felt the same need to see it for himself. Of course, I had previously witnessed the crash scene when I went looking for Corbin, but the circumstances were now very different.

Jeff measured how far up the tree the car had hit and also the distance between when the car left the ground and went airborne. After the reconstruction team investigated the accident, we would learn that the car was traveling around a hundred miles per hour. It went airborne twice, for between seventy and eighty feet each time. The vehicle careened directly through a smaller tree before striking the massive oak tree that ultimately stopped it. There is no saying how far the car would have continued had the hulking oak tree not instantly halted its travel.

On our way to Boston, Paul called us. He had driven straight to Boston from the hospital in Concord, and he had been in contact with Boston Children's Hospital (BCH) on his way down. They almost lost Corbin several times during the flight and needed to rush him back into emergency surgery as soon as they landed.

It's a very helpless feeling to learn that your child is so close to death and you have absolutely no control over it. Part of being a mom is having the innate ability of being able to fix everything that is broken in your child's life. Nothing is beyond repair, whether it is a broken toy, a skinned knee, or a schoolyard bully that is treating your child unfairly. Those things are easy to resolve and come second nature to all good moms. The realization that Corbin's body was so broken and there was nothing I could do to repair him, left me feeling extremely powerless.

That ride to Boston felt never ending. I watched the minutes tick by in slow motion. I couldn't stand the sense of anticipation, and yet, I was dreading what I was going to hear if the phone rang before we arrived. We arrived at Boston Children's shortly after Paul did, so he met us in the lobby and brought us up to date on what he had learned about Corbin's flight down. He showed us to the waiting room on the ICU floor that Corbin would be brought to after surgery.

Despite our earlier request to refrain from rushing down to Boston, most of the family and even some of Corbin's friends were sitting impatiently and waiting with us. I couldn't be angry as they were there to support Corbin and me, and it was comforting to know that they were there with us.

Corbin's new night nurse came in and introduced himself as Jay. I will never forget how amazing he was from the second he introduced himself. He calmly and confidently explained that he would be in frequent contact with the operating room and promised to update me as often as he could. He was kind, compassionate, and I immediately knew this wasn't just a job for him, but his passion. Meeting him and seeing how much he truly cared, gave me another shot of confidence that, somehow, Corbin was going to make it through.

Right after Jay left the room, BCH's transport crew came into the room. Paul had worked at BCH on that crew for about ten years. When they learned that his family was involved, they showed up to offer their support. They even took Corbin's younger siblings down for a tour of the ambulances. They returned with toys and coloring books to keep them occupied and their minds off of their brother.

We also had visits from child life specialists and social workers, each who took care of us emotionally, while the medical team was trying to save Corbin physically. The social worker brought us towelettes to try to refresh us and helped everyone that would be staying to book hotel rooms for the night. The TLC we received before Corbin was even out of surgery was so far beyond what I would have ever imagined. I knew we were in good hands and, suddenly felt that if anyone could save Corbin, it was going to be the staff at Boston Children's.

Corbin was in surgery for about four hours before a man walked into the waiting room wearing scrubs. He was the neurosurgeon who had been working on Corbin. He wanted to personally explain to us the details about the new combination monitor and drain that he put into Corbin's skull. He said his brain was going to continue to swell for some time. This can actually cause a secondary injury in addition to the damage his brain had already sustained. The monitor would give the team the notifications they needed so when Corbin's brain swelled, they could react and drain some of the fluid out. This would provide the brain with the space it needed to prevent any additional damage.

Of course, we all had a million questions for him, but he explained that another surgeon would have to explain the rest. He could only give us the information that pertained to his portion of the surgery, but he assured us that everything went well. He told us that Corbin was actually thrashing around when he got there which led him to believe that his brain was injured but it wasn't dead.

Jay came back in and told me and Jeff that Corbin had been moved up to the floor and we could go see him now. He warned us on the way down the hall about what to expect when we saw him. I thought, *We've already seen him. We know how bad he looks.* Boy, was I wrong. We were brought to the far corner of the floor, which was pretty open with three patient spaces separated by a pull curtain.

I later learned that this is where the sickest patients go so that they are all in the same area if they need immediate emergency treatment. They also told me that Corbin was by far the most critically injured patient that they had had on the floor for quite some time. This wasn't how I wanted Corbin to gain notoriety.

When we saw Corbin, somehow, he looked worse than he had initially. His temperature was high, so he didn't have a gown on, just a sheet from the waist down. His left shoulder, where they had been removing the glass, looked like it had been through a meat grinder. Both of his eyes were black and swollen shut. His entire face was swollen and distorted.

His stomach was not stitched up in order to leave room for his internal injuries to heal. So, he was left wide open from his pelvis to his ribcage with a bright blue sponge and several drains protruding from it. He honestly looked like some roadkill that had been hit by an oncoming eighteen-wheeler and left out for vultures to nibble at the rotting carcass. He had bloody gauze hanging out of his nose and blood was flowing from his ears resembling an IV drip.

As vividly as I remember these catastrophic images, I'm being totally honest when I say that it didn't faze me. As horrific as it was to see my child like this, there was a huge sense of relief to be back beside him, knowing that his body is still warm and fighting to remain alive. Jeff and I both cried. We were also so happy to be touching him and reassuring him that we were at his side and he was going to be okay. Though Jeff and I would struggle in the weeks and months ahead, for a moment at least, we were unified and pulling in the same direction for our son.

People will often report that hearing is the last sense to go when someone is severely injured. I've learned that it is important to talk to people who are unconscious, because even though they can't respond, they can likely still hear. There may be no visible reaction, but they may be able to hear. Even if that wasn't the case, we were still going to talk to our son. We didn't know if his brain was functioning at all, but it didn't matter. If there was any of him in there, he was going to know that he wasn't alone, and we were there to get him through this together.

4

MEETING THE TEAM AT BOSTON CHILDREN'S

Not long after they let us in with him, they told us the trauma doctor and his team wanted to have a meeting with us to go over the surgery and their proposed plan moving forward. About twelve of us, not including the doctors and nurses, gathered in a small conference room on the ICU floor; a room that was better suited for about half that number. They proceeded to tell us what was done in the operating room, including the addition of a second monitor and drain in his skull. They repaired more internal bleeding and replaced the wound vac in his abdomen, which would remain open from his rib cage to his pelvis until they were confident they could close it.

He was put on additional medications to stabilize his vital signs and had another CT scan, which showed severe hemorrhaging in his brain. Lastly, they inserted drains in both punctured lungs. As if that wasn't enough, they added that he had two broken shoulder blades, a broken collar bone, multiple skull fractures, multiple facial fractures, and several spinal fractures. The litany of injuries seemed endless.

At that point, I didn't understand at all how he could still be alive. Everything on that child seemed broken, and anything that wasn't broken was severely damaged. They continued to talk about his injuries, but the conversation always came back to the brain damage. Broken bones heal, punctured lungs heal, you can live without a spleen, but you can't do any of it without a functioning brain.

The doctor explained that the brain doesn't heal the way the rest of the body does. He was also still at risk for greater damage to his brain in the coming weeks. He explained that Corbin's brain was going to continue to swell and that they wouldn't be able to guess at the extent of the damage until the swelling ceased. As the brain swells it can put so much pressure on the brain stem that it could put him into a vegetative state or even kill him.

Despite, the somber tone and the desperate nature of the explanation, it still felt like better news than the first hospital had provided. As awful as his condition was, they weren't giving up hope and had a plan as to what the steps were to produce the best possible outcome. No one told us that it was time to say goodbye as the neurologist had dropped on us in Concord. It was all very devastating, but it was abundantly evident that they were going to fight for him and do everything they could to produce the most positive result. The goal wasn't to allow him to die quietly but was to aggressively help him survive. For me, that was enough for now.

The majority of the family in the room that night asked the doctor the same question in twenty different ways. We all wanted to know what his chances were. We all needed to know about his chance of survival, his chance for a full recovery, and his odds of being our same Corbin again. As unlikely as that may have seemed at the time, none of us had accepted the fact that this was going to have anything but a miraculous ending.

I believe that this ignorance was a key part of Corbin's prognosis. We refused to accept the fact that he was going to die. If he wasn't going to die, then we refused to accept that he was going to be anything but whole again. Perhaps that was wishful thinking but that's how we committed to going about this.

That's when we first realized what a waiting game it was. As quickly as Humpty Dumpty was broken into pieces, it was going to take much longer to put him together again. We needed to be patient and resilient and understand what that meant. The medical team kept saying that we have to wait and see what Corbin does, how he reacts, how he recovers. He had health and youth on his side and those were our two positives.

No one can predict the future and when I look back now, I realize that the doctor's wisdom helped me immensely. That's how I looked at everything from that point forward. I know Corbin better than anyone, and I know what he's capable of. He's a born fighter, and if anyone can do this he can!

After the longest day of our lives came to a merciful close, everyone started to go their separate ways. Most drove back to New Hampshire, while some went next door to the hotel rooms that the hospital had set up. We gave Corbin's sisters, Mari and Grace, and cousin Tanna an opportunity to see him if they wanted to before they left for the night. Tanna was of course in the accident with Corbin. Somehow, he only suffered minor spinal fractures and some cuts and bruises so he was released before Corbin was even out of the first surgery at Concord.

Tanna was in the waiting room with all of us when the doctors came in and the neurologist had informed us that Corb wasn't going to make it. He may have been the most devastated of all upon hearing that news, and he insisted on coming to Boston that night with his parents. He stayed with my mom in her hotel for the first week that Corb was there so he could be with him as often as possible.

To this point, only Jeff and I had seen him. Most of the immediate family who were still there were adults, and even they weren't ready to handle it. We didn't even give Cohen the option. He was only ten years old, and we felt that he could be traumatized for life seeing his brother in that condition. We reassured him that Corbin was being taken care of and everyone was doing everything they possibly could to make him better.

His sister, Mari, and Tanna wanted to see him, but Grace decided that she wasn't ready. Corbin, Mari, Tanna, and Grace were together all the time. Though they were not family by choice, you would have thought the four of them grew up together. Corbin and Grace were best friends, only twenty-two months apart and practically inseparable. They were so close that she knew she couldn't handle it yet. It's pretty amazing the things we do to protect ourselves without even realizing it.

I knew she wanted nothing more than to be by his side, but how do you prepare yourself at age fifteen to see someone who means so much to you in that deplorable condition? It's really incomprehensible. No matter what you've been through, nothing in life can prepare you for seeing a child, brother, grandson, cousin, or best friend in Corbin's state.

We all handle these situations very differently depending on our personalities or our relationships with the person. Mari and Tanna felt like they needed to see him. I believed that it was important for everyone to take this at their own pace, so I took them back. I'm sure what they saw that night is burned into their minds forever. I tried to prepare them for what they were going to see, but that isn't remotely possible. They looked petrified before they even entered the room. It's one thing to hear someone explain what he looked like, but it is completely different when you see it with your own eyes.

They stood beside his bed, absolutely speechless. They were afraid to get too close. Afraid to hit a tube or wire that was attached to him and keeping him alive. They looked like two little kids walking into a china shop after their mother lectured them to not touch anything. Corbin looked so fragile that you didn't even want to breathe wrong for fear of breaking the delicate thread that had him hanging between life and death.

I wondered if he could really hear us. I wondered if he was in pain. Worst of all, I wondered if this would be the last time, we'd all see him alive. The kids blankly stared at him in disbelief, with their mouths hanging slightly open and tears streaming down their cheeks.

By this time, it was about 2 a.m. so we made it a quick visit for Mari and Tanna before I brought them back to the waiting room. Steve and I said goodbye to everyone and prepared to head to Corbin's room. Even Steve hadn't seen Corbin yet. He was as apprehensive as everyone else to see how bad Corbin really was, but he handled it well.

I stood and looked at Corbin with one hand over my mouth and chin while nervously running the other hand through my hair. At that moment, I realized everything it was taking to keep him alive. He had two tubes coming from his mouth, one for breathing and one to drain his stomach. He had a drain tube coming from each lung. He had another tube coming from his open stomach and another protruding from his skull. At that moment, he looked more like the bionic man than he did my son.

The number of pumps and machines surrounding him was intimidating to say the least. His body was littered with drains and IV lines, blood transfusion lines, and medicine lines, as well as heart monitor lines and temperature probes. I didn't know where I should touch him. I needed to be close enough so that he knew I was there. I needed him to feel my hand on him and to hear my voice like when I spoke to him through the bathroom door as he prepared to go out tubing. At that moment, that conversation seemed so long ago and eerily prophetic.

When I was being a mother and telling him to be careful, I was encouraging him to be cautious on the river that day. Never in my wildest dreams did I envision that he would never even reach the water. Sometimes a mother just knows. It was unfathomable that this was the same day that began with me not wanting to roll out of bed. How I wish I had pulled the blankets over my head and refused to participate in the day that would unfold before me.

Our nurse, Jay, was so amazing that night. He reassured me that it was fine to get close to Corbin, to touch him, and to talk to him. He just looked so broken. It seemed like anywhere I touched him would hurt or would cause him to disintegrate like a sandcastle at the beach with the tide rolling in. He had blood oozing from his ears, his nose, and his mouth.

His left side, where I was standing, had sustained the most severe injuries. It was the side that had the broken collar bone and shredded shoulder, yet somehow his hand appeared unscathed besides some dried blood around his nail beds. By now it was about 3 a.m. Jay never left Corbin's side either, intently watching every number changing on the multiple monitor screens and making constant adjustments to ensure that Corbin was as comfortable as possible. I felt very confident having Corbin under his care.

It was a roller coaster ride to say the least. I don't know how many times Corbin began to crash that night. His blood pressure would drop, then his temperature would spike. He fought the breathing machine with his own breath. Every time those machines would start screeching, no fewer than a dozen members of the medical staff would come rushing in and surround him to ensure that it was nothing catastrophic. I would jump out of the way as I saw them stampede in every time.

They would tell me not to move but stay right beside him. So, when this would happen, I would hover over him, putting one hand on his chest and one on his face. I would whisper to him to try to relax. I would say, "I know you're scared, but you're going to be okay. I'm right here." Eventually, Steve noticed his heart rate and breathing would slow down when I started doing that. That felt like a huge sign to me.

He was alive inside of his smashed and broken body. Even though the lights weren't shining brightly, there was indeed someone home. Something was working inside that he could hear me, feel me, or sense me in some way. I knew at that point I couldn't leave his side. If I could have any positive impact on keeping him here, I was going to do everything in my power to remain by his side constantly.

I can't count how many times that night it was touch and go. Jay kept asking me if I wanted a chair so I would sit but I couldn't. I stood by Corbin's side, leaning over him throughout the night. I don't know how I was still standing upright but I couldn't reach him as well when I was sitting. Eventually, Jay ignored me and brought chairs anyway. I kept telling Steve it was fine for him to sit. He didn't need to stand with me all night. Eventually he agreed and dropped exhausted into his chair.

After asking me multiple times, Jay came around the bed and pushed the chair up behind me. He begged me to sit for just a minute. As soon as I sat down, he lowered Corbin's bed to a height that I could sit without losing contact with him.

Before the shift change the next morning, we got our first experience with "rounds." First a large group of men and women, the neurosurgeons, came into the room like a herd of buffalo and started talking extremely loud to Corbin. "Hello Corbin. My name is Doctor Strong. Can you hear me, Corbin? Can you wiggle your fingers?" Nothing. "Can you wiggle your toes?"

I glanced down to Corbin's uncovered foot and saw his big toe move slightly. I screamed, "That's it! He's here! He can hear us, he's responding!" The team of doctors didn't quite have the same reaction.

Right after his toes moved, everything started going haywire. Jay realized all the commotion was agitating him. His heart rate skyrocketed, and his blood pressure plummeted. Doctor Strong and his team believed his toe movement was only a reaction to what was going on in his body and not him responding, but I felt differently. Granted they are surgeons at the best children's hospital in the world, but they don't know my son. They didn't see his earlier reactions and responses. I refused to believe them and returned to my new mantra, "Sometimes a mother just knows."

After that, we met about twenty different doctors and specialists who came in to assess Corbin. Neurosurgeons, neurologists, respiratory therapists, trauma surgeons, orthopedic surgeons, ophthalmologists, and the list goes on. The crew who had worked with him throughout the night was the evening shift, but now as night turned into day, the heavy hitters were beginning their rounds. We saw all kinds of doctors that day, many with specialties that I had never even heard of before then. Jay remained with us, and I can't even begin to explain how attentive he was. He seemed to know what was going to happen before it started, and he had everything on the ready to stabilize Corbin the second anything changed.

At that point, it was clear that Corbin needed to be in a more private room where all of the noise didn't bother him. I kept thinking about the amount of pain he must be in. His whole body was destroyed. I wondered if he was resting pain-free until the noise disturbed him, causing him to feel it all. These were the things I wondered throughout the day seeing him in that condition. There is no worse feeling in the world than seeing your child bloody, broken, and fighting for life and not being able to take their pain away.

I felt so utterly helpless. I prayed even though I don't customarily turn to prayer. I tried to bargain with any higher power even if I wasn't sure what I believed. I would literately give my own life to save his and make him whole again.

The following morning, I sent a group text to the family to bring them up to speed. I felt that communication was necessary and frequent texts would not only keep them from worrying but would also keep my phone from ringing endlessly.

The text read:

So, nothing but good things all night. He's had a lot of movement on his own and with stimulation. A minute ago, he grabbed my hand, pulled it right off the bed and continued to squeeze it. He's moved his shoulders, bent his knee, and wiggled his toes. He still has a breathing tube to assist if needed, but all the breaths he's taking are on his own.

They keep giving him mild sedatives as they believe he's having these reactions because he's starting to come to and is in pain or stressed, but basically becoming more aware. Jay said he really does think he's hearing us the way he's reacting. I thought it would be nice to wake up to something positive, so I wanted to share the positive news.

As helpless as I felt, I never gave up hope. I tried to see every positive, as minuscule as it might be, and ride the wave of momentum. I may have made the text sound slightly more positive than the reality, but this was how I chose to view the situation. Glass half full as opposed to broken and leaking all over the table.

I found myself playing the role of mother, nurse's assistant, public relations person, and cheerleader all at the same time. If I could do nothing else, I was going to will him better in any way I could. I made up my mind at that point that the positive was all I was going to focus on. It was the only way I thought either of us were going to survive this.

Around 7 a.m. our new nurse for the day, Rosa, walked in to get an update from Jay. I was petrified to see Jay turning the care over to someone else. Jay had taken such good care of Corbin that I didn't want anyone new providing an inferior level of care. Jay had not stopped moving the entire night and I couldn't imagine that anyone else would provide Corbin with the same level of attentiveness. The amount of equipment and machines Jay was managing to keep Corbin alive was something you had to see to believe. He reminded me of the circus entertainer spinning plates in unison and not allowing a single one to stop spinning, let alone crash to the floor.

Even while giving Rosa the report he didn't stop moving or

leave Corbin's side. I wondered how she was going to take all this in. How is she going to take this in without missing some piece of critical information; vital information that she may need in order to keep Corbin progressing in the right direction? But she did. She jumped right in like she'd been there all night. She got us moved to a private, quiet room right away and, little did I know, that she was soon to become part of the Raymond family from that day forward.

5

OUR FIRST STEP ONTO THE CARINGBRIDGE

By this point, it had been twenty-four hours, and I couldn't keep up with the influx of messages from family, friends, customers, or friends of friends who had heard what happened. I felt awful. I didn't have time to keep checking my phone to send out individual messages to what seemed like hundreds of people. I didn't want to leave Corbin's side. Everyone meant well and were utterly concerned, but I needed to focus on Corbin and not on being a public relations agency.

Paul walked in bright and early on the fifth of July, and I started explaining this to him. He told me about a website where I could post updates, and everyone could read them. One message a day or once a week; whatever I had time for. It sounded like the perfect solution.

I hadn't been on social media since my divorce and really liked my privacy. There were so many parts of my life that haters could troll me on and critique that I had opted to lay low and out of the limelight some time ago. Currently though, I knew I needed an outlet to update people. So many people cared, and I felt they deserved to know how he was doing.

I signed up for the site called CaringBridge and wrote my first post. It was extremely difficult to write, yet very therapeutic at the same time. CaringBridge became a great outlet for me and ended up playing an invaluable role, not only in keeping people informed but also in allowing me to vent and heal emotionally at the same time.

There was something else that was really bothering me, as well. The day before as we watched Corbin's helicopter take off, Grace told me that she was hearing rumors that the driver of the car was getting bullied and receiving threatening messages. That upset me so much. I've always had a tendency of putting myself in someone else's shoes. How would I feel? How would it make me feel if I had been the driver of the vehicle and started receiving threats? There was no doubt that he felt bad enough about what had occurred and what could potentially still happen. He certainly didn't need this hanging over his head on top of everything else. I knew I needed to set this straight.

Corbin's friend Tyler was the driver of the car. Tyler and Corbin had been friends since elementary school. Tyler was at my house two to three times a week since they were eight years old. I cared about him, and I didn't want this taken out on him. These were teenage boys and though it was pretty clear that they were speeding, there was obviously no ill intention. Reckless? Yes. Foolish? Absolutely. But if he could have that moment of teenage mischievous behavior back, I knew he would. Corbin got a speeding ticket the week before the accident, and all I could think was it could have just as easily been him driving.

Later that day, I reached out to Tyler's mother. I told her that we loved Tyler and we didn't have any hard feelings. I told her what I had heard about kids giving Tyler a hard time and asked her permission to post something about it. I told her that I wouldn't use anyone's name because the people that I was speaking to know who they were and who they were gossiping about.

She gave me the okay to share the post and said they were praying for Corbin. I needed to finish the post to send a message to everyone who was waiting for updates. Little did I know, when I published that first post, the magnitude they were ultimately going to have to everyone who was gravitating to our story.

My first post read:

As many of you know, Corbin was involved in a serious car accident on the Fourth of July. Corbin and his friends were planning a fun day of tubing down the river. The details of the crash are all hearsay to us at this point. Corbin was rushed to Concord Hospital, where it took a while to stabilize him, and then he was rushed into surgery. We were told he had severe head trauma and bleeding in his abdomen. They were going to operate but couldn't give me many answers because they had to open him up to find out the extent of his injuries.

When they came out of the OR, they told us that his injuries were catastrophic, and he would not recover because of the brain injury. We were devastated. Shortly after, a doctor came out and said a few things had changed. They were seeing some positive signs of brain activity. Luckily, Corbin has a family member (Paul Raymond) who has been our lifesaver. He is in the medical field and suggested that we get him flown to Boston Children's Hospital because it is a Level one trauma hospital and would be best equipped to treat Corbin.

Within an hour, the helicopter was there, and he was airlifted to Boston where he immediately underwent two more surgeries. As of now, he's touch and go. They still don't know the extent of his injuries. They have been doing everything they can to keep him stable and right now the main goal is to monitor his brain for swelling because the first forty-eight to seventy-two hours are the most crucial. Corbin is sedated and has had his family by his side as much as they allow.

We appreciate everyone's thoughts, prayers, and kind words for Corbin. We can't express enough thanks for everything Boston Children's Hospital has done for him and is continuing to do for him. It's really unbelievable, and we know he's in the best hands here. It's hour to hour right now and we will try to keep posting when we have news. The last thing I really wanted to say is that these kids involved were all young and any one of them could have been driving. We know all of these kids and care deeply about all of them.

This is a time to pull together because all of our families are struggling in different ways. The last thing I want to hear is that anyone is blaming anyone or that anyone is getting bullied or blamed. We don't feel this way AT ALL and don't believe anyone else should. We also need to remember that these kids involved were some of Corbin's best friends, and he would have no respect for anyone treating his friends poorly.

When I wrote that first post, I'd been awake for at least thirty-six consecutive hours. Thirty-six of the worst nightmarish hours imaginable. No sleep, no food, no hairbrush, no makeup and, I hate to admit it but, not even a toothbrush. I certainly wasn't at my best mentally, physically, or emotionally. It took me hours to write that initial post. I would start sitting by Corbin's side while he was having a quiet moment. All I got was a few uninterrupted moments in the beginning where I'd write a sentence or two before a machine started frantically beeping. He would then start fighting the breathing machine and it looked like he was convulsing.

Doctors, nurses, and Steve would encourage me to eat something and to go take a shower. Eating wasn't an option. I felt terrible and food was the last thing I could possibly think of. I know they had my best interest in mind, but a vending machine snack or a greasy helping of fast food was the furthest thing from my mind. Steve had gone downstairs to the cafeteria and got a small variety of things I might like. I tried to take a few bites, but it didn't feel right. I couldn't bring myself to take care of myself when Corbin was hurting so much.

Shower? Not a chance. I don't know if my son is going to live or die, and you expect me to leave his side to SHOWER?!? Not a chance of it. I probably could have broken down and shoved a little toothpaste in my mouth, but even that little bit of hygiene didn't seem necessary.

I sat on the chair next to Corbin's bed and went into a daydream that was likely fueled by a combination of exhaustion and delirium. I looked at my severely broken son and traveled back in my mind to his birth sixteen years earlier. I likely dozed off unknowingly as my thoughts took me back through memories from Corbin's birth.

Corbin was my first child. The pregnancy was a surprise that came only a few months after Jeff and I were married. At the time, we bought some land and planned on taking some time to build our future home. We knew we wanted kids, but Corbin put our plan into fast forward. We were living in a tiny, cheap apartment that I really didn't want to bring a new baby into. So, we hired a builder and got the house moving. I was working a customer service job at the utility company, and Jeff was selling furniture at my mother's furniture store.

The pregnancy was absolutely exhausting. After work, I would come home at the end of the day and barely make it to the couch. I'd fall asleep for a few hours, with my jacket and shoes on, until Jeff got home. Then, I would get up, cook dinner, and go straight to bed. I had no energy at all. Aside from that, it was a pretty uneventful pregnancy.

Corbin was due on August 22nd and our one-year wedding anniversary was August 26th. The due date came and went. Like most mothers that make it to their due dates, I was absolutely done. Nine months pregnant in the middle of the summer added to my desire to get this child out of me. He was cooked and perhaps even a little bit overdone. I knew he wasn't a little baby, and I felt like I might explode if he got any bigger.

I had decided to use a midwife for my care and delivery with Corbin. Little did I know that they didn't like to induce labor, so we waited and waited. I had an appointment on the 29th, one full week overdue, and I prayed they would take me to the hospital and get things moving.

To my displeasure they said to give it a few more days. I just about lost it. I felt like I couldn't do it any longer. So, Jeff took the rest of the day off, and my water broke at about 2 a.m. Thirty-six hours later on 9/1 Corbin was born. His birth date was 9/01/01 or 911 we'd joke. At that point, I should have known what this kid was going to do to me.

The labor was very long and painful. He was facing the wrong way so his skull was pressing on my spine, where normally his face would be. It's called back labor and it was excruciatingly painful. I took no pain meds and at no point did I consider changing my mind about that. I wanted no chance of it affecting him or my ability to take care of him after he was born.

The labor was so long that my body shut down. My contractions stopped twenty-four hours into labor. They needed to give me medication to start the contractions again. I couldn't eat and hadn't slept in forty-eight hours.

The next step was to get the operating room ready. My water had been broken for so long, Corbin was at risk of infection and my body had given up on pushing him out. I begged not to have a C-section, so they gave me a little more time and the Pitocin worked. Contractions started and Corbin was finally here. All nine pounds and twenty-three inches of him.

I was petrified to bring him home. I had only held one other baby that little before, and now they wanted me to bring him home and keep him alive? I was scared I wasn't feeding him enough. I was scared that people coming in the house would make him sick. I didn't want to bring him in public. You might say I was crazy overprotective.

I soon realized that I had been staring at him for several minutes thinking of his entry into the world, and I wondered if he would survive long enough to add even another memory to my mental scrapbook. I snapped back to reality and continued squeezing the hand of my broken son.

6

NOT SURE HOW TO KEEP IT TOGETHER

My second post would come a bit quicker than the first as I witnessed the positive impact it seemed to have on everyone who read it. People that we knew were brought somewhat up to speed instead of wondering or hearing things through the rumor mill. And, oddly enough, people I didn't know immediately began following our story and offering well wishes and prayer. As I made it clear previously, we aren't big prayer people and don't make religion a huge part of our lives. But in a case like this, we were grateful for every prayer that was sent in our direction and graciously received every one of them.

The second Journal Entry was posted two days after the accident on July 6th. Though only forty-eight hours had passed since the accident, it seemed like weeks. It wasn't until I typed in the date July 6th, that I realized it had only been two days and not a lifetime as I had originally calculated.

Friday Journal Entry — July 6, 2018

Corbin made it through the night with stable vital signs and no new issues. We've made it past the forty-eight-hour mark, which is huge but still know the next twenty-four are equally dangerous. Even though he is under heavy sedation, he has shown us a few more positive things today like wiggling his toes and trying to cough when they suctioned his breathing tube. He becomes agitated when they move him around but responds very well to Mom and Dad talking to him to calm his heart rate and breathing.

They plan on doing X-rays on his limbs to check for broken bones this afternoon. Luckily, they come right into the room to do that. He continues to have stable vital signs, and if everything continues to be stable, they are hoping to try surgery to work on a few things on Sunday. We are so thankful for all the support we're getting from all of you. We tell Corbin about all of it!

It is pretty incredible that your child can be lying there in front of you with who knows how many broken bones, and yet that is not the prime concern at the moment. The doctors are so focused on monitoring the pressure in his brain and keeping him stable and alive that the broken bones are merely an afterthought. Things you would normally rush a child to the hospital for, like a broken arm or leg, sit on the back burner until the more pressing issues are addressed. It's almost as if they disregard the broken bones since a leg or an arm is of little importance if the brain is not going to survive.

This entire experience helps me to put things into perspective. Things that seem so important on one level have suddenly become insignificant. Things like broken bones, taking a shower, even eating, are far less important than holding my son's hand, rubbing his forehead, and letting him know that we love him. Keeping him alive is the only thing that matters. A clean house, clean hair, and a healthy meal are at the bottom of the to-do list and will remain so forevermore. All that matters is our health, our love, and our family remaining intact and alive.

At this point, we are a few more days in and my level of exhaustion has reached a whole new level. The doctors keep telling me to go outside, get some fresh air, take a shower. These menial tasks feel impossible because they mean leaving Corbin's side. I would leave his room to use the bathroom, only when absolutely necessary, but that's it. Even then, I tried to hold everything until the last possible moment, which at times was not the smartest idea.

Just like I was a known procrastinator filling my gas tank, I had now waited until the last minute to empty my tank as well. Anything I ate or drank was brought to me. I would sleep for an hour here or there in the middle of the night when specialists weren't coming in to examine him. I believe this was the first day they convinced me to shower. I have to admit that it felt really refreshing, and likely necessary, even though I didn't stay under the warm soothing water for very long.

Steve and I had been in the room night and day. Jeff, Angie, Cohen, and Keira were staying at the hotel next door, and my mom, Grace, and Mari were staying at a nearby hotel. The hospital gave us a family room to sleep in with a community bathroom to share with other ICU families. I never had any intention of sleeping in there, but I knew a warm shower would eventually be needed. Jeff had shown up as he usually would before anyone else had arrived for the day so he could spend some alone time with Corbin. Alone, except for me of course, who wasn't going to leave Corbin even to give Jeff some privacy with his son.

For the hundredth time I was told to leave the room for my own sanity. Steve suggested I shower (which may have meant that I had passed my expiration date and it was *really* time for me to shower), and then we should go to the room to sleep for a little bit. Jeff assured me that he wouldn't leave Corbin's side and would call me with any changes at all. I reluctantly agreed. Though Jeff was Corbin's father and perhaps very capable for the short term, I was his mom and wasn't going to leave Corbin under the supervision of anyone less qualified than me. Call it selfish or stingy or even holier than thou, under these circumstances that's the way it was going to be.

The family room was in a different section of the hospital but felt like it was miles away. I had a few random articles of clothing I had thrown in my backpack before heading to Boston. I grabbed some leggings and a sweatshirt, my flip-flops that I'd been wearing for days, and some trial size shampoo the hospital had given us. The bathroom was cold and didn't feel private at all. When the water first hit me, it felt like such a complete relief. I let the warm water spray against my face and stood there for several minutes letting the dirt, as well as a bit of stress, come off of me and swirl quickly down the drain.

That was the first time in days that I took a deep breath in and out. That feeling was fleeting. As fast as the feeling came, it was replaced with a strong wave of guilt for not being by Corbin's side. The guilt was then quickly displaced by a sense of anxiety and panic. *What if something went wrong and I couldn't get back to him fast enough? How can I be thinking of myself at this time, while my son needs me? What kind of mother would leave her son while he clings to life?* I quickly turned the water to off and jumped out of the shower as fast as I could. After a quick towel off, I got into the leggings and sweatshirt, and then I rushed back to the family room where Steve was.

The room was extremely tiny, smaller than a dorm room with a cot size bed. Steve tried to reassure me that nothing had changed with Corbin. He was fine and in good hands with Jeff or else we would have heard something. I knew the exhaustion was taking its toll on him just as it was on me. He asked me to lay down with him and rest. I tried but I was extremely restless and likely a bit overtired. I made sure the volume on my phone was as loud as it could go, and I held it in my hand like a child with a teddy bear as I tried to relax.

I would dose off momentarily and wake up startled, dreaming that I had missed a call. I couldn't relax. I couldn't stay that far away from him. I wasn't trying to get some sleep for my well-being. I was trying to please everyone else and to get them to stop insisting that I have some downtime. In retrospect, I know I needed to get some sleep and know that they were looking out for me, but at the time it only made me feel worse.

The shower didn't help, laying down and getting out of the room didn't help. I felt like my heart was outside of my body, beating so loudly that the world could hear it, and I wasn't going to survive a minute longer without getting back to Corbin's room. I sat up and whispered to Steve, who had fallen asleep. I told him that he could stay and rest, but I needed to get back. I ran back to the room as fast as I could, slightly panic-stricken. Nothing had changed, neither positive nor negative, but I felt relief as soon as I was back in the room.

Day number four brought another CaringBridge Journal Entry, which I sat and wrote as Corbin lay next to me of course. As before, our following was getting larger, filled with familiar names of friends and family and the names and comments of friends we'd yet to meet. The media covered the story of the accident pretty heavily, and messages of support and prayers of hope were coming in from all over the state and the New England region.

Happy Morning - Journal Entry — July 7, 2018

Corbin has pulled through another critical night with stable vital signs. The doctor that told us he had a fifty-fifty chance of making it through the night, two nights ago, came in and said, "He's doing it. He's surviving!" He also said that he believes Corbin has made it through the most dangerous period for brain swelling. He will get a CT scan today to look at his spinal cord and his head again. They have no images of his spine, so they don't know the damage there yet. The doctor also told us that both shoulder blades are broken, and he has a broken collar bone, in addition to broken bones in his face that we already knew about. At this point, they don't see anything else broken in his limbs. We know we're not out of the woods by any means. There are still so many risks, but we're taking it hour by hour. We know Corbin has so much to still overcome, but like his dad said, he's a fighter and is still fighting hard!

As I wrote this, I thought of the doctor's words and though I was never much of a gambler, a fifty-fifty chance of survival seemed like shockingly low odds. A coin flip chance to make it through the night after all he has already been through. How can that be? I believed that if he survived that first night, then he's out of the woods! I bargained with myself constantly. I would not let myself think negatively even when I didn't like what the doctors were telling me.

Corbin survived the night after the accident, even after we were told to say goodbye. He somehow survived the flight to Boston despite almost losing him. He made it through two emergency multi-hour surgeries. All of this led me to feel a lot more positive about how we were progressing. Then the doctor came in, said he's done well, and now he's got about a punchers chance of surviving through the night?

That felt like the worst gut punch you can possibly imagine. Just when you think you've made it through the worst of it, they tell you "Well, the next seventy-two hours will be touch and go because the most damaging swelling happens in the first seventy-two hours." Jesus, when are we going to be able to breathe a little easier?

I sat and gazed at him as I had for the past three days. I still couldn't get over how broken he looked. The black eyes, the swollen face that made him almost unrecognizable. He still had blood draining from his ears, and cotton swabs stuck in his nostrils drenched in blood. He looked like a deer that a hunter had shot, killed, and tied to the roof of his vehicle to transport home. I couldn't fathom how much blood he must have lost.

His hair was absolutely matted and caked in dried blood. Corbin had been growing his hair out and finally had "flow" as he liked to call it. He was so proud that it was long enough to finally pull it back in an elastic. Now, he had two big shaved spots right in the front where the monitors and drains were drilled into his skull. Though it likely would have been the least of his worries, I thought about how he would be devastated to see that all that of his work to grow his flowing locks was out the window in an instant.

His stomach was still wide open from his ribs to his pelvis. His internal organs had experienced so much swelling that they didn't dare close him up. His spleen had been removed, and there was a drain coming out of the gaping hole in his abdomen. He had drains coming out of him everywhere, tubes in and out of him. The machines surrounding him looked like something you might think was over-exaggerated in a movie. I bit my nails until they were bleeding, worrying about how much pain he might be in.

I asked the medical staff constantly if they thought he was in pain. I was always assured that he was under so much sedation that he wasn't feeling any of it. What about if he woke up? I couldn't even fathom how much pain he would be in. They also assured me he wasn't waking up anytime soon.

By this point, family and friends had really started to step in more than we could have imagined, to help us pick up our lives where we left them earlier that week. We had other children. We had animals, jobs, homes, and bills. I gave my notice at the bar on the day of the accident, as I knew that I wouldn't be back any time soon. This would be a long-term commitment and serving drinks to strangers and discussing their petty problems was the least of my worries.

My cousin, Jenn, who was also my closest lifelong friend, worked with me as well. She tried valiantly to sweep up the pieces of my life. She looked for people to take care of my cats, found a friend to take our dog, and picked up my shifts at the bar. All of this was in addition to trying to be with me at the hospital in Boston as much as she could.

Grayson was still with Steve's mom and sister, where he had been since Wednesday. They were getting ready to go on vacation to a rental home on Lake Sunapee that Saturday and luckily agreed to take Grayson with them. Cohen had been staying next door in the hotel with Jeff and Grace. They were in the same hotel as my mom, so at least I was able to see them every day.

I know by this point that Steve was really missing Grayson. It had been four days since we'd seen him. It wasn't that I didn't miss him too. I missed all of my kids and tried to remind them that I love them with all my heart. But I couldn't focus on anything but being by Corbin's side, willing him to heal. I knew everything and everyone else could wait. It was a dire situation and that's all I could handle.

Doctor Mooney came to be my daily alarm clock, waking me at the same time each morning and providing me with the plan for the day. He came in and seemed to have a very positive attitude about how Corbin was progressing. He also gave me his daily speech about getting out of the room and taking care of myself so that I could be strong enough to take care of Corbin. I would smile and nod agreeably while saying under my breath, "There's no way in hell I'm going anywhere, Doc!"

Well, that day Steve took the opportunity to ask more directed questions and push me to leave for the day. He had already decided that he was going to leave with or without me to go see Grayson at the lake. I thought that was great. He needed it and I was fine with him going, but I didn't need to go. He really wanted me to join him, so he encouraged Doctor Mooney to convince me that Corbin was stable enough for me to leave.

He was quite sure nothing serious was going to happen. Jeff was also in the room and, as two men often do, he jumped on the bandwagon. It's difficult enough to stand up when double-teamed but more challenging when they were both your husband and significant other. I felt bombarded and said I would think about it. After Jeff and the doctor left the room, Steve pleaded with me, so I seriously considered going. Corbin was having a CT scan soon however, so I wasn't going anywhere until he was safely back in his room. They really wanted to close his stomach as the risk of infection escalated every day.

Moving Corbin out of his room for anything required strategic planning. Any movement of his body made his vital signs go nuts. He was attached to so many pumps and machines, and it all needed to be transferred to mobile devices. It took a team of many doctors and nurses to make it happen. Three people were needed to push poles with medicine pumps. They told me that I could stay with him for most of the trip. It was terrifying. I joined the caravan once everything was transferred to the battery-operated machines and the CT team was ready for him. They never made me leave his side until the very last second and said they would allow me to return when it was safe for me to be around him.

I went down the hallway like I was part of the medical team and even squeezed into the elevators when there was no room. They never rushed me when we finally reached the point that I had to leave his side. I was living every moment of my life in fear that it was my last moment with him. When it came time for the nurses to wheel him in to perform the procedure it was heart-wrenching. I would try not to get too upset in front of him. He would be upset if he saw or heard me get distraught. I would do my best to kiss him, tell him to be brave and that I would see him in a few minutes.

The second the doors closed I was alone and that's when I would absolutely lose control of my emotions. That's when the break my heart fear would set in and the realization that it could be the last time, I ever see my son. I was working so hard to be strong and positive for Corbin and the rest of the family, but I was crumbling inside. Whenever I had a few minutes to myself, with no one to witness how bad I was hurting, I'd let my hair down and melt into a puddle of mush. I realized that an occasional cry wasn't a bad thing, and it actually made me feel a bit better. I would give myself a few minutes to fall apart, collect myself, fix my face (though I was really fooling no one), and then head back to his room to muster up a smile and wait for his return.

The doctor let me know that he didn't handle that CT very well. They had to move him from his bed onto the machine bed, and his vitals went berserk. His heart rate skyrocketed, and his blood pressure dropped. They had a really hard time keeping him stable. He was down there for quite a while as they attempted to get him stable enough to get him back to his room. Once he was back, he settled down and was fine. Doctor Mooney assured me it was the physical move that was difficult for him and that he still wanted me to leave the next day.

The surgery they hoped to do was going to have to wait. He needed more time to heal before risking another move. He said they probably wouldn't have results of the CT scan until Monday anyway. He explained that nothing was going to be done to him that day. No tests no procedures, only rest so he gets stronger. Once again, at the doctor's order, I reluctantly left Corbin's side. We went next door to the hotel where everyone was staying. Mari and Grace were also going to head to the lake and my mom, who had driven to Boston with us after the accident was going home for the night. I tried to convince myself that it was going to be okay.

Doctor Mooney wouldn't have told me that I could leave Boston for a few hours if he didn't think Corbin was going to be okay, and I had come to trust Doctor Mooney. He didn't sugarcoat things. He told me how things really were. He would allow me to feel positive about the good but would also be straight forward as hell and tell me he had only a fifty-fifty chance of survival. Even though his brutally honest approach hurt at times, I needed to have a realistic understanding of where things stood. I could continue to be optimistic but at the same time I needed to know the potential challenges we were facing at all times.

He told me from the start that they could fix Corbin's body and bones. He was young and healthy, and as bad as he looked from the outside, that was all healable. His brain was a different story. They don't know everything about the brain. The brain doesn't heal at the same speed as the bones. The brain takes much longer.

He had seen kids with less severe injuries not survive, and he had seen kids with injuries that were as dire as Corbin's make remarkable recoveries. As silly as this phrase may sound, the brain has a mind of its own. We had to give Corbin time, and let him show us how he was going to play the hand he'd been dealt.

Maybe, I was justifying it in my heart and my mind, so the guilt of leaving him didn't eat me alive. But if Doctor Mooney said it was going to be okay for me to leave for a while, I decided to trust him. My mother was, of course, also a proponent of me leaving when we got next door to her room. Steve had a renewed positive energy. He was so excited to see Grayson. We told the girls that we would be going up north also, and everyone seemed more positive. I thought maybe this family getaway was a good idea after all, as it lifted the morale of the entire family.

Untitled - Journal Entry — July 8, 2018

They did find quite a few fractures in his spine, but that's the least of our worries right now. Neurology came in and told us that they are very concerned with the lack of brain activity they are seeing. They are pretty confident that he will have some permanent brain damage. We won't know the extent for a long time. None of us are giving up hope and are trying to focus on the little positives we're getting in other areas.

This post took everything I had in me to sound positive and unfortunately, I think I failed miserably. I had started to feel an obligation to update everyone as if they were sitting in front of the computer, tapping their fingers in anticipation, waiting for an update. I felt like even though I was feeling as broken as Corbin inside, I had an obligation to look after the health and emotional well-being of everyone who was being so thoughtful and support-ive. I felt that I owed them upbeat and positive communication so that they didn't worry unnecessarily.

Granted it took me well over twenty-four hours to gather the strength to write, but I still felt like I needed to do it. I've been accused of being a nurturer and caring about others more than I care about myself, and I guess those accusations were justified. I promised that I would try to think of titles for my posts, and that day I had nothing left inside. This post would forever go through life nameless. I had finally concluded, without anyone telling me, that I was starting to run on fumes, and if I didn't begin to take care of myself, I wouldn't be able to keep up this pace.

The day before, just as I was starting to think maybe a few hours away wouldn't hurt, Jeff texted me and asked where I was. I told him that I was at the hotel with the girls getting ready to take a few hours away. He asked me to say nothing to them, to not react, and to come out of the room into the hallway. Steve and I left the room together and saw Angie and Jeff walking down the hallway. Jeff was visibly sobbing.

Jeff and Angie had stayed with Corb after Steve and I left for a few minutes. I thought to myself, *WHAT THE HELL?!?! What possibly could have gone wrong in that brief amount of time? I had been gone only twenty damn minutes!* I looked at Jeff, who physically was a big hulk of a man. At this moment, he appeared much smaller than normal and could barely speak. Angie spoke for him and said they were saying goodbye to Corbin for the afternoon when the neurologist came into the room.

He told them they just looked at the CT scan, and they were seeing no brain activity at all. They didn't think that he was going to regain consciousness. He should be showing some activity even under heavy sedation, and their fears by seeing his lack of physical reactions were proven by the scan.

I heard Angie retelling me what the neurologist had just told them, but I went numb again and could not comprehend her words. I immediately went into shock and began to scream. Hands in my hair, I shook my head from side to side and began to scream and sob. "No. No. NO!! What about the progress? What about fifty-fifty odds?" I started rambling and spouting off a litany of rhetorical questions.

NOOO! I wasn't accepting it. I had left for twenty minutes and this happened! This is why I didn't want to leave to begin with. I shouldn't have let any of these people talk me into leaving. I should have been there with him. I would have asked questions and had gotten better details. I would have argued until I received a better outcome because there was no way this was going to play out like this.

We went into my mother's room since all the kids were in Jeff's room. I looked at Steve and did a complete 180. "I'm not going anywhere!" The family looked at me like a had two personalities. Jeff suggested we go back over so we can ask more detailed questions and get some solid answers. He then asked Steve if he would come with us. He believed that Steve may ask things that we might not think of since Steve wasn't as connected to Corbin. That sounded ridiculous to me as Steve had been in our lives for five years and certainly had become attached to Corbin. He was as upset as any of us, but that wasn't the time for me to question Jeff though, so I just bit my lip.

The four of us went back to Corbin's room. I asked the nurse to call the Neuro doctors back. I had begun to have ill feelings toward this group of neurosurgeons and the neurologist, just as I had in Concord. They gave little information, and when they did it was always negative. I dreaded their daily exams. They seemed to offer no glimmer of hope, only doom and gloom. I was mad about everything at that moment.

I was mad that I left. I was mad that I let anyone talk me into it, and extremely mad at those damn doctors for having provided us with such awful information. Who did they think they were? They don't know everything. They can't guarantee that he'll never have brain activity. Who are they to play God with my son?

At a perfectly timed entrance, before I exploded, a female resident walked in. She was quite young, about post-college age, and worked on the neurology team. She explained what they look for in someone Corbin's age and what they believe based on the test results. She didn't sound nearly as sure that he would never regain function as Jeff and Angie had interpreted. Now don't get me wrong. She certainly didn't have good news and didn't provide us with a sense of overwhelming hope, but she didn't say anything that I perceived as guaranteed despondency.

I felt one hundred percent better when she left, and we all

did. Jeff explained their experience was with the head neurologist who had explained things very differently. Whenever I spoke with him previously, he seemed to be extremely intelligent but lacked the bedside manner needed to acknowledge the fact that he was giving information to frantic grieving parents. So, I accepted the fact that we didn't have good news, but it wasn't as bad as we thought an hour ago.

We went back to the hotel and brought my mother up to speed. Everyone insisted on carrying on as we had planned for the day which though hard for me to admit, I understood to be necessary. We went to the food court, grabbed sandwiches for the ride, and started the trip back to New Hampshire. Though I should have felt a temporary sigh of relief and a bit closer to normal, I felt numb. I was completely out of sorts not being in the hospital, my new home away from home.

I had taken a few bites of my sandwich when I got a message from Jeff's sister, Christine. It was intended to be a note of encouragement, but it hit me really hard. I began sobbing uncontrollably. I couldn't eat as tears streamed down my face for two solid hours. It was as if the dam of emotions that I had been holding back for nearly a week, all broke at once and flooded everything in its path. We dropped my mother off and I cried some more.

By the time we got to the lake my tear ducts had likely dried up. I composed myself just in time to walk through the door and have Brenda, Steve's mom, hug me. She hugged me tight, and I could feel her genuine love and concern leave her body and enter mine. She asked how I was holding up and the floodgates opened again. I was a sobbing mess once more.

Despite Steve and I reaching the end of our five-year-long relationship, I had always liked his mom so much and felt like we were very close. I knew that when Steve and I parted ways after the dust had settled, I'd lose her also. She made me a drink and brought me out by the water to try and see the positive light. This was very typical of Brenda.

Grayson was loving the lake. He absolutely blossomed in the water. He was seeing fish and turtles and was as happy as could be, protected from the nightmare the rest of us were living. Sometimes, I wish I could bottle his childlike innocence and sell it on the open market, or at least take a swig myself. As adults, it would be powerful to find a way to care about nothing but fish and turtles while the world is crumbling around us.

I ended up pulling it together pretty well the rest of the day either due to the serenity of the lake or the incredible healing power of one of Brenda's drinks. We played with Grayson and watched the older kids enjoy themselves to the best of their abilities under the circumstances. It was therapeutic for all of us to get away from the hospital for a bit, frolic, and enjoy a great meal.

As soon as it started to get dark, I began to get really anxious to return to Corbin. We hadn't received any calls from the hospital, and I only called three or four times to check in. The reports from the hospital were good, but I needed to be back by his side for what was left of my own sanity. We said our goodbyes and left for Boston.

Steve and I seemed to have overlooked the fact that we were breaking up, and he was supposed to be moving out on the day of Corbin's accident. We both loved each other very much, but we just didn't work as a couple. Our bad days highly outweighed our good days, but when something like this happens you just don't walk away. Steve cared for me, and he cared for Corbin and the rest of the kids. He'd been in our lives for almost five years, and I don't think he wanted to leave Corbin's side any more than I did.

It didn't take long before our issues resurfaced, however, despite the fact that Corbin's situation was attempting to play referee between the two combatants. On the ride home I told him that Jenn wanted to start a GoFundMe account and to hold fundraising events at work to collect money to help pay bills. I explained that it made me feel somewhat uncomfortable. I know that crowdfunding has become commonplace in today's world, but it made me feel like we'd be begging for people's money. I never wanted people to view me in that way.

He listened for a few moments and then went to DEFCON 1 without ever stopping between five and two. He screamed, "How dare people start something like that without our permission." That's not where I was going with the discussion at all. I appreciated the good intentions but didn't want to look like I was asking for money.

Well our difference of opinions, our lack of sleep, or our distance from anything resembling sanity got the best of us. Especially me. Before I knew it, he was raising his voice at me. I started screaming back at him to stop yelling at me, and then I lost it. I screamed and cried, and I started slapping his face. I saw rage! "How dare you yell at me at a time like this," I screamed. I hit him three or four times before I realized what I was doing.

He reacted by doing nothing. He didn't try to stop me. He didn't stop driving. He just looked straight ahead and said nothing. I was ashamed and embarrassed but wasn't able to control my emotions. I knew that I had lost control. I shouldn't have done it, but I didn't feel less angry. I had snapped under the pressure of everything going on, and I'm glad that I regained composure enough to stop when I did. I never knew what it felt like to be in a fit of rage, but that is as close as I ever want to be.

I ordered him to bring me to my car and that I didn't want him back at the hospital. I didn't want him anywhere near me now or ever again. He continued in silence and just looked straight ahead at the road. I knew he was seething inside, but he wisely kept his composure rather than poking the wounded mama bear. We rode to Concord Hospital in silence where my car had been parked since the day of the accident. I texted my mom and asked her to come with me back to Boston. Of course, she agreed with no questions asked. I got out of Steve's car, slammed the door, and Steve sped away.

I was delirious. I put my car in what I thought was reverse and drove straight into the concrete wall in front of me. That was the only thing separating me from the twenty-foot drop to the ground below. That felt like a wakeup call until I shifted out of park and did it again.

I fell apart entirely. How was this my life? How was I going to survive? I managed to back up and make it to my mom's place, as I don't think I would have been able to make that drive back to Boston without her by my side that night.

7

THE SMALL HURDLES

We got back to BCH around midnight, and I didn't even go to the parking garage. I went straight to the entrance and handed my keys to the valet. I didn't know or care if I was supposed to do that. I just knew that I needed to be in that room as soon as possible to see that Corbin was still there, warm and alive. After a wonderful day, followed by a terrible night, I wasn't going to let anyone else convince me to leave his side until we left the hospital together.

When I got upstairs all was good and quiet. That was the moment I realized how much the smell of iron from all the dried blood in his hair, the beeping of the machines, and the air rushing in and out of the ventilator oddly gave me so much comfort. I was like a fish out of water when I wasn't in that room. I needed those sounds and that horrible smell to assure me that I was with my son and that he was still holding on.

I felt so much more relaxed once I was in there. I hugged

Corbin and kissed his forehead. I assured him that Mom was back, told him his siblings were doing well, and reminded him that he was going to be fine. I told him he was defying the odds and that we needed him to keep fighting. Though he didn't acknowledge my words verbally or even with anything resembling body language, I knew that the boy inside his shattered body could hear me. He was doing everything he could to obey his mom. I crashed for a few hours after one of the more challenging days of my life.

When I woke up in the middle of the night, the episode with the neurologist from earlier in the day was eating at me. *What if they were right? What if he never wakes up? What if he's in a vegetative state for the rest of his life? What if he's never able to hug and tell me that he loves me again?* My mind was overflowing with anxiety while unanswerable questions were flying at me faster than I could attempt to field them. Each time I calmed my mind momentarily, I worked diligently to think of another question to bother me. I let those thoughts get the best of me and mustered up enough energy to write a journal update once I got out of bed the next morning.

Quick Message - Journal Entry — July 8, 2018

Corb had a good day. Stable all day, no spikes in vitals. That's all we can ask for at this moment. He had a PICC line put in with no complications. They can get him nutrition and emergency medicine with this line so it's a good thing! One more quick message I've been asked to post. People are donating to this page, and I guess some are confused about where the money is going.

This page asks for money to keep the updates coming, but it's a free page for us. We did not set this up for donations! We know so many people care about Corbin and want to know how he's doing. I know how hard it is not knowing when someone so special is hurt. That's the only reason we set up this page. Any donations made go to the website not to us. Obviously, do as you wish, but we aren't charged to do these posts.

At this point, I felt like my life was flying at me in warp speed. I felt like I was the target in a video game of Asteroids. It seemed like everyone and everything was bombarding me from every direction. Family members were trying to help in every way, and I was appreciative, though a bit overwhelmed. They came up with several ideas to raise money. We all had other children that needed to be taken care of as well as homes, animals, and jobs. All in all, most of that was taking a back seat, but we were extremely grateful that our family jumped into action to take all of those concerns off of our plates.

They started a GoFundMe account to raise funds, were diligently trying to design bracelets and sunglasses they can order and sell to raise money, and they were even talking about having Corbin Strong T-shirts made. Of course, they wanted Jeff's and my approval for everything before firming up designs on their projects. So, as I sat there watching my child fight for his life, I still had to deal with normal life. Add on all these extra tasks as well and it is mind-boggling.

It was taking everything I had in me to be strong and making decisions about bracelets or T-shirts simply wasn't something I could add to my plate. Grace and Mari stepped up and took on the roles of bracelet designers. It was a good task to keep them occupied and made them feel like they were doing something to help. They say it takes a village, and our village certainly came through in flying colors. There was enough work for everyone to take on and an army large enough to leave nothing incomplete.

Being outwardly strong was taking its toll on me and what had happened the night before indicated that. I'd never lost control and hit anyone before, and I felt bad about it. In some ways it may be understandable, as no human mind can take on all this added pressure and hold it together, but physical violence against someone you care about is really not who I am. Steve had started texting me first thing in the morning.

He'd still driven down to Boston and couldn't find a nearby hotel with any rooms, so he slept in his truck. That made me feel even worse. I asked him to come back to the hospital. I was so overwhelmed. Corbin's accident alone was enough to completely submerge me, but a failed relationship, grieving children, and an uncertain future in so many regards were enough to break me.

The Small Hurdles - Journal Entry — July 9, 2018

Corbin was stable all night, which meant that surgery was a go. He had a lot done today. The most important was closing up his stomach from the internal wounds. The rest of the surgeons were waiting to see how much he could tolerate before they knew if they could proceed. Closing his stomach went very well. The doctor was very pleased to see all of the previous repairs were as they should be, so he felt comfortable closing the incision.

The next issue was trying to determine if his broken collar bone actually came through the skin during the accident, which would put him at risk for infection. It in fact did, so they opened that up and cleaned the area but didn't repair the break. Next were the oral doctors who were looking for sources of bleeding. They cleaned the nasal passages and mouth of blood clots but didn't have to stitch or cauterize. Lastly, was a visit from the eye surgeon who wanted to check his eyes for debris, glass, or bone

*fragments. One eye did get a small incision, but nothing was found. The
area of concern is believed to just be a bruise.*

*Corbin made it through all of it with stable vitals and brain pressure
for the most part. The doctors were all very happy with the outcome. He
would not be fast-tracked to fast food as he would probably like, but Corb
is finally on some liquid nutrition as of tonight and off of the medication
to stabilize his blood pressure, as he's now taking care of that himself.*

*These last few days have been a nightmare roller coaster. We get
over these hurdles like surgery today, they tell us his body is healing well
and his chance of survival is going up every day. We also have neurologists who continue to report doom and gloom about his brain function.
They remind us that we have decisions to make down the road due to
the quality of life he could have because of the brain damage. So, we
continue to live in the right now, hang on to the positives, and have faith
that Corbin's going to pull through this.*

*Once again, we want to thank everyone from the bottom of our
hearts for reaching out with your similar stories that have positive outcomes, the kind words and prayers, sending us food so we can stay on the
floor and not have to go too far from Corbin, and our family for picking up
the slack at home or helping with childcare. We can't thank you all enough.*

It blew me away that the doctors didn't yet know the extent
of all of Corbin's injuries. He hadn't been stable enough for all
of the tests, X-rays, or exams to find out. The focus, for now, was
solely to keep him stable and alive. He could be lying there with
four broken limbs but that's secondary when the brain damage
is so severe. At this point, both of his eyes are black and swollen.

One eye is so swollen that it bulges out farther than his forehead. They tried to examine it, but the fluid needed to dilate the
eye would react negatively with other medications. Also, every

time they tried to open his eye and shine a light in, his vitals would spike, and they would need to stop. Once again, a secondary concern when you're just trying to keep him alive.

Besides having his spleen removed, he had so much trauma to his organs that it was necessary to leave it open to let all the swelling go down. Under most circumstances, it wouldn't be open for this length of time. He hadn't been stable enough until now to tolerate the surgery necessary.

This surgery was scary and was going to last for hours. There were teams of doctors from different fields that were going to take turns working on him. So much of our family was in Boston with us still. Even more came down, knowing that the surgery was likely going to occur on that day.

Once it was time for surgery, the team of nurses and doctors piled in to transport him to the surgery floor. I couldn't help but worry about the chance that it could be the last time. The last time I might get to see him alive, the last time to hold his warm hand, or the last chance I'd have to say I love you. So, I walked beside him, I talked to him and told him that he was going to be fine. I never said goodbye. I only said, "I love you, and I'll see you soon." I tried to hold it together as much as I could until he was out of sight.

Once he was wheeled away, a nurse walked me down to the floor where we would wait for updates. I tried to control the tears as I gave them my phone number to call when he was done and then wandered to the elevator in a zombie-like condition. I sobbed as I rode alone back to the ICU waiting room where everyone was waiting. I walked in and everyone looked to me for information. I had no update. No news either positive or negative.

I was merely a shell inside my body. In some ways Corbin and I were complete opposites. He was a totally destroyed physical body with a spirit inside that was trying to fight long enough to recover. I was a perfectly fine physical body with a wounded spirit inside trying to hold it together long enough for him to show signs of survival. Together we were one. Apart we did not equal the sum of our parts.

We all went our separate ways. Jeff and Angie went to their hotel next door, Steve went to my mom's hotel room to try to sleep for a little bit, and Grace and Mari had some friends down to visit so they went next door to Starbucks. Mom, Jenn, and I went to the hotel restaurant for three healthy glasses of wine. Hours passed with no call from the hospital. No updates. We were roused from our girl talk, when the nurse finally called and said that Doctor Mooney would like to see me.

I panicked and felt like I screamed into the phone, though likely I wasn't as loud as I envisioned. "Is everything okay? What's wrong?" She said, "He'd just like to talk to you in person, rather than over the phone." I couldn't breathe. Something happened. I know it did. The worst thoughts were running through my head. I looked at my mom and said, "I need to go!"

The hotel was next door to the hospital. I started running as fast as I could to get there, weaving in and out of people like a Patriots running back. I called Jeff on the way and told him. "Why did he need to see me in person? Why couldn't they tell me over the phone that he was okay?" I hung up as shortness of breath, from my anxiety and running through the halls in flip-flops, was making it nearly impossible to talk on the phone. It was bad. It must be something bad. My God, how can we make it this far and it just end like this? This can't be happening.

I don't know how I found the waiting room that I had seen so briefly through tear-filled eyes earlier. I ran to the desk, shaking, quivering. I asked for Doctor Mooney, and they advised that he would be down shortly. This made the few moments before he arrived nearly unbearable. I couldn't stop picturing him coming in and telling me the worst news.

Doctor Mooney came in minutes later, before Jeff or anyone else had arrived. He walked me to a private room and started to explain what the team had performed on Corbin and how smoothly everything had gone. I almost didn't believe what I was hearing because I had worked myself into such a state of hysteria. What a relief! I couldn't believe it. He was okay. He was stable through Doctor Mooney's entire surgery.

I thanked him over and over. I wanted to hug him but didn't know if that extended beyond normal patient/doctor protocol. He told me that as the other teams finished, they would be out to fill me in. I came out of the room walking on air.

It was amazing, but understandable, how emotion was able to get the best of me. I went back to the waiting area where everyone had finally arrived. Grace and Mari were there with a look of sheer panic in their eyes. They were sitting outside of Starbucks with friends and saw me run out of the hotel and toward the hospital, so they had run after me. Steve was there, too. Jeff and Angie had seen Steve in the hall and told them Corbin was out. They were all expecting the worst as well. How could they not?

They had all been in the room when they told us that we would need to say goodbye. They had all seen Corbin's fragmented body lying in that bed with machines keeping him alive. We were all hanging on by a thread of hope as we knew Corbin's life was barely hanging on by that same tiny fiber. I shared the good news, though I was hyperventilating slightly and was having difficulty forming words. Everyone sobbed in relief when I told them that he had made it over yet another hurdle.

The next hour and a half was difficult. Corbin was still in surgery, and despite our renewed sense of optimism, there was still a chance of it going the other direction. The teams came out one by one to give their updates. The eye surgeon told us they flushed the eye, made a small incision, and found nothing. They also said that they were able to get the first good look and believed he would keep his eyesight in both eyes.

The next team was there to examine his left collar bone, which we knew had been broken by the seat belt. As it turns out it was broken in two spots, and in one of those areas the bone had punctured his skin. That meant a chance of infections, so they opened the area and cleaned it out. They chose not to do any more than necessary and did not repair either of the breaks. They believed the breaks would heal on their own. If they needed repair in the future, we would deal with it down the road when he was more stable.

The next team was there to examine his mouth and throat. There had still been a lot of blood coming from his mouth and other areas. Everything had been so swollen that it had been hard to tell where it was actually coming from. They found no significant areas that needed repair, so more good news. With each visit by the next team of doctors we would cross another area of concern off the list and would breathe another sigh of relief. No high fives yet, but certainly cause for optimism.

At this point, Corbin had been only on clear IV fluids for nutrition, so after making it through everything that day they decided it was time to put him on some real nutrition. It was a huge positive step. How can your body heal and repair itself with no nutrition? It felt like a big win for the day, but just when we felt like we were taking two steps forward we became accustomed to getting shoved five steps back. I guess that's why they keep encouraging us to live in the moment and celebrate the small victories.

The neurologists would come in a few times a day. Every time I saw them approach the big glass doors to Corbin's room, I would get a sick feeling in my stomach. It was like they were there to burst this little fragile bubble of goodness that had been inflated during the day. They would run their battery of tests on his reflexes. It was never enough. They wanted to see more. More movement, more reaction from Corbin and, with each day that passed, their outlook and demeanor seemed to get nastier.

I'd hope for some improvement neurologically so that the team would give me a reason to get excited. With each passing day, Corbin stayed pretty much the same in their eyes, and their reaction made me physically ill. I dreaded their presence, and they were beginning to recognize that. I interacted with every doctor that came in the room. I wanted to know everything they were doing and why.

With this group however, I would simply watch them do their tests and silently wait for them to leave. I was convinced that they were wrong in their assessments of Corbin's brain activity, and I didn't need to hear any more negativity. They didn't know Corbin. They didn't know his laid-back personality or how easily medication affected him. To them, he was a medical case and not the boy I had witnessed every day for the first sixteen years of his life.

I told myself that he wasn't reacting because he was so sedated. I didn't care that they were likely some of the smartest doctors in the world, they didn't know my son. I'm sure I sounded desperate and crazy when I'd argue with them, but I needed to believe in Corbin in order to stay strong. I needed to stay strong for Corbin and for the little bit of sanity I had left.

8

ONE STEP FORWARD, THREE STEPS BACK

When it quieted down each evening, I would sit on my makeshift windowsill bed and check the hundreds of hearts and comments people would leave on Caring-Bridge. The amount of love and support people showed would blow me away. People had the kindest words of love, hope, encouragement, and prayer. Strangers left messages about similar experiences they had been through, each with positive outcomes. It all made a huge difference for me, and it gave me the strength I needed to keep going and to stay positive.

After I read the hundreds of daily messages, I would take my phone and sit by Corbin reading him the messages. I wanted him to know how many people were thinking of him, how many people cared about him. Any little thing I could think of to give him the same strength that I was trying so hard to muster up. I needed him like I needed my own heart. I needed him to fight and to come back to us.

Day 7 - Journal Entry — July 10, 2018

Today Corbin was weaned off of the sedation. It was stopped a few hours ago, and now we're back to the nightmare waiting game to see if he will regain consciousness. It's pure torture. He had a few things done, like rolling him to his side, chest X-ray (in his bed), and he was taken off of the blood pressure medication as well. The majority of it he handled pretty well. I write these posts when I get a quiet minute to sit down at night. On the one hand, it's a struggle for me because I'm kind of a private person. On the other hand, I know so many people care so much about all of us. Everyone wants Corbin back and healthy, and that means so much to us!

All I can say is, what I write doesn't begin to explain the extent of how bad Corbin's condition really is. The doctors say that he's young and healthy. From the chest down they can fix with time, but he has injuries I haven't even touched on because his brain function is the priority right now. So, we sit and wait. We're playing his favorite music, telling him stories, and telling him how famous he's become with all the people who love him and check this page to see how he's doing. Thank you everyone, for the continued support.

Day seven feels more like year seven. How is it possible for time to move so slowly? Minutes feel like hours, hours feel like days, and days feel like years. I've never wanted to fast forward time, before now, because under normal circumstances the faster it moves, the older I get and who wants that? People suggest taking in every minute, but I didn't ask for these minutes. I didn't want anything that went along with them.

I wanted to dream, to believe that this nightmare was going to have a happy outcome. I was playing a heart-wrenching game of wait and see with no answers anywhere in sight. The neurologists had seen this before and I hadn't. They had a much longer history of seeing signs and determining the likely outcome. I, on the other hand, knew my son. My goal was to do anything I could to bring him back. I put together a list of things that I wanted to bring from home, like his pillowcase, blanket, and deodorant. Jenn gathered them up and brought them to the hospital during one of her many trips back and forth between my house and Boston. She made that trip almost every day in the first three weeks.

Corbin's choice in music isn't one you would normally hear in a hospital, never mind an ICU, so I would take my phone and lay it on his pillow near his ear to quietly play Metallica. Now that is an oxymoron if there ever was one. Metallica is only intended to be played at one level of volume, and the album *Hardwired to Self-Destruct* is not conducive to the ICU. But again, we made alterations to what may have been considered the norm.

Corbin's cousin Paul had been at the hospital with us from the beginning. He would also make that trip daily. His presence and knowledge of the industry were so reassuring. We had so many doctors and specialists in the room every day talking about treatments, medications, and possible outcomes. It was overwhelming.

I had worked in hospitals and had some experience, but Paul understood so much more than I did. He was our medical translator. He always stayed calm and transferred that calm demeanor to me. The moment Paul came in and saw the phone by Corbin's head, he got an idea. The next day he arrived with a small tablet to play music on, so we weren't draining our phone batteries that we needed to keep family updated.

Longest Week Ever - Journal Entry — July 12, 2018

For the moment things have slightly slowed down. We were hoping for some signs of brain activity and petrified to not see any. After a few hours of the sedation being turned off last night and about forty-five minutes straight of talking to him and telling him stories, he hadn't budged. I laid down in the back of the room and thought it was just too soon to see any response.

Of course, as soon as I closed my eyes, I heard a noise and flew out of bed. He was trying to cough on his own. They rushed in and suctioned his lungs which agitates him, but he was also twitching and trying to move his shoulders as if saying, "Leave me alone." I was told these were all good signs. As the night and rest of the day went on, he had periods of unstable vitals and high pressure in his head. Corbin has two machines placed in his skull to monitor the pressure and drain excess fluid.

Being so unstable he was given more pain meds and sedation to keep him calm. This meant we didn't plan on seeing much as far as brain activity today. That's what the majority of the day was like, just sitting around watching the nurses adjust meds to keep his vitals stable. When his dad was leaving to get lunch, he asked him to blink for different reasons. After about the third time Corbin tried to blink and then moved his head and shoulders. We all felt pretty amazed that maybe he's hearing us and he's still in there.

That's about all we got today. We're told the numbers are fluctuating because he could be starting to become more aware without the sedation. So once again we hurry up and wait. He's been sedated a few more times, so I'm not sure if any signs are in the cards for tomorrow.

I watched the numbers on the monitors reading the pressure in his head religiously. I watched his temperature, his blood pressure, the breathing machines, and the medication pumps intently. I watched the canisters collecting fluid from his stomach, lungs, and head. I knew what the fluid color should be, and I became aware when it was too little or too much. I knew what every machine was for and every medication he was on. I watched how he reacted to each of them.

Nothing in his body could regulate itself. The majority of the time they had this torturous cooling blanket on him to keep his body temperature down. It was a full-length mat filled with water, and it was hooked up to a machine that controlled the temperature. I didn't understand why it wasn't giving him frostbite. I would sit next to him and have to wrap a warm blanket around me because the cold coming off of his blanket made me freezing even being near it.

Corbin loved sports. He knew every statistic of every player. Sometimes I accused him of being a walking/talking sports encyclopedia. He watched each trade rumor diligently, and he had loved to fill me in on every bit of it daily. We had essentially switched roles as I was now providing his daily sports update. I found websites with every trade and contract detail. I would sit and read them all off to him.

The biggest deal he had been waiting for was the Lebron James contract signing. He had told me that he thought Lebron would be leaving the Cavaliers. I found out about Lebron's decision to leave Cleveland and told him that he was going to have to start wearing an LA Lakers jersey. I wanted so badly to see his reaction.

I didn't know if he was hearing anything that I was saying. I didn't know if there was even a shell of the former Corbin sitting in front of me, but I refused to believe that he was gone. I know he was simply resting long enough to heal and that once he was well enough to return to his former self, he was going to open his eyes and surprise us all.

One Step Forward, Three Steps Back - Journal Entry — July 12, 2018

The eighth night went like the day with random spikes in blood pressure and inner-cranial pressure. I saw the pressure in his head climb to the highest I've seen since the accident. Eventually, everything seemed under control, so I went to the back of the room to sleep until about 4:45 a.m. when they said they needed to bring a CT scanner in the room to check his head. What a terrible way to be woken up!

When the doctor came back in to discuss the results, he said that they saw no changes and the swelling in his brain hadn't gone down like they hoped it would. So once again, a new plan of action. We're basically back to day two post-accident, as far as progress with attempting to find out the brain damage. Corbin has been put back on full pain meds, sedation, and a sodium solution that helps reduce the swelling in his brain. The doctors and nurses have spent all day trying to get him stable.

His blood pressure is still higher than they want, and he's spiked a fever. Everything else is higher than it has been but not in a dangerous range. Currently the plan is to stabilize him and let him rest a few more days before trying to come off the meds. It's never-ending. As I sit here writing this, they changed the attachment that sticks to his face to hold his breathing tube in place. Then they suctioned his lungs through the breathing tube.

I actually have started to enjoy watching this because his nostrils flare, and it makes him try to cough on his own. Right now, that's the tiny bit of life we get to see from Corbin. So, we continue to wait . . .

I again found myself traveling back in my mind to Corbin as an infant. We moved into our new home two weeks after he was born. I refused to put him in his nursery. I couldn't bear for him to be out of my sight. I had a security company come and quote an alarm system because I overthought everything. I felt that the only way he would be safe, was if my house was locked tight like Fort Knox.

Corbin wasn't the easiest baby. He hated the car. He screamed from the second he got in his car seat until we took him out. Often with our short twenty-minute drive to the grocery store he would scream so much that he would make himself sick and throw up. So, I would have to change him, then feed him so he was nice and full before we went in. He still would end up screaming in the store, and I would have to leave a full shopping cart and try again the next day.

He would let very few people hold him without crying. When he was a toddler he would hide when new people came to the house. He was shy and quiet when other people were around, but he was simply saving his crazy for us. He had a little temper!

This kid was my life. He made me a mom. I spent the last sixteen years protecting him and I had no control now. I felt like a shell of a person. Like part of me was dying inside but giving up or thinking negative thoughts wasn't something I would ever do. I didn't picture myself going back home without him or to his empty bedroom.

I didn't allow myself to imagine what Christmas morning would be like without him, or all of the things he might not be there for. Especially, with Steve soon to be vacating the house, Corbin was involuntarily promoted to "man of the house." Although, his role would be far different than Jeff's or Steve's of course, our house still needed a male that was older than ten at the head of the dinner table.

Some days, it was so hard not to feel defeated, but until he unexpectedly takes his final breath, I am going to keep fighting. There was no other choice in my mind. I knew that he was still barely clinging to life. No one had any idea if he would even wake up, but you don't stop fighting for your children.

It was a good feeling knowing that the doctors and nurses were fighting just as hard. Rosa and Jay were becoming like family. They worked twelve-hour shifts and rarely left Corbin's side. The majority of their alternating half-day shifts were spent in the room with us, right by our side. They advocated for Corbin and were becoming just as over-protective of him as I was.

His recovery was out of my control. So, I clung to the little things that I could control. Things that would make him feel better or so I hoped. I knew they made me feel better as his mom and sometimes that was half the battle. I would put Chapstick on his lips, cut his nails, and put lotion on his peeling skin. I bought a baby brush and would gently try to work around the monitors and drains in his head to brush the remaining cakes of dried blood out of his hair.

My brushing would destroy the clean pillowcase below his head, but the staff never acted irritated by my actions. They always listened, made suggestions, and dealt with my nonstop presence and my endless stream of questions. Rosa tried to get our room switched to one with a private bathroom and a working TV after watching me have to use the bathroom or brush my teeth in the public waiting room bathroom. She knew that I wanted to turn the TV on a sports channel for Corbin so he would never be alone.

Jay had been like a guard dog protecting Corbin from day one, and that was all I could have asked for. He never pushed me to leave or go outside like the doctors would. He had children of his own, and he understood my need to be around Corbin. He would wrap a warm blanket around me on the nights I fell asleep in a chair with my head by Corbin's side, instead of waking me up and ordering me to lie down.

I had all the trust in the world for these two, and I felt bad for the random nurse that would have us when neither Rosa nor Jay were working. I knew too much. I knew how everything worked, what agitated Corbin, how his body position should be, how to move him given his fractures. Anyone new became very aware of my role in the first five minutes that they had Corbin for the day.

9

I'LL NEVER TAKE IT FOR

GRANTED AGAIN

Thank You - Journal Entry — July 13, 2018

Sometimes, as I write these updates, I fear they won't make much sense when I read them the next day. I usually write them when I'm beyond deliriously tired, so I'm starting a little earlier tonight. Corbin had a pretty stable day. He does have a fever they keep trying to figure out and keep under control. His vitals are on the high side of safe, but he's stable.

Both chest tubes have been taken out, and his chest X-rays look good. At this point, we can't ask for much more. He's fighting, and his body is healing. His head just needs more time. We have actually gotten out of the hospital the last few days with the other kids, so he has quiet time and gets the rest he needs. He's super sensitive to any stimulation.

I wanted to take the time to thank everyone tonight. My family, Jeff's family, Steve's family, Angie's family, all of our friends, neighbors, people we work with, and even people we don't know who have reached out to us. We read all of the messages and try to respond. Even if we don't, we appreciate your love and encouraging words. It gives us the strength to be strong knowing that we have this amazing support system from all across the country. People are sending food, taking care of our homes and animals, babysitting, sending gifts, donating to GoFundMe, and sending flowers and gift cards. We are blown away with the outpouring of love for Corbin and our families, and we're so lucky to have all of you.

The continued support was amazing. It was really mind-blowing. I can understand the outpouring for the first few days when everything was new, and everyone was in a state of concern. The fact that the number of page views and the number of followers continues to grow into the tens of thousands is a lot to comprehend. We aren't famous. We come from a Podunk town in New Hampshire, yet our story is being watched across the country and in many other countries.

It's a lot to take in. I'm so private and have such a small circle of close friends. I'm always so shocked by the kindness and generosity of everyone. It really helps me in so many ways.

Our lives before the accident weren't perfect by any means. Jeff and I had been divorced for over four years, and we had new relationships for about the same time. Our families grew as we both had young children with these new relationships. Despite being divorced, Jeff and I had gotten along fine until the last few years. Even through our divorce, there were no lawyers. We shared a very basic parenting plan because we wanted what was best for everyone.

We figured between our schedules and three young kids we would make it up as we went along. That didn't last too long though as Corbin and Grace didn't get along with Jeff's new wife,

Angie. In some ways, this is perfectly understandable. Many times, when a parent gets remarried the kids give the new spouse more than they signed up for. After many discussions with no resolution, both of the older children asked to live with me full time as they just didn't like the atmosphere in their dad's home living there on a part-time basis.

The relationships between the two homes became very strained. Corbin was the most adamant about not even visiting his father's house unless it was a holiday. Corbin and Grace were very hurt by the strained relationship with their father. Corbin once came home from a birthday party at Jeff's house, after not being there for a while, and told me they have a whole wall full of family pictures and he wasn't in any of them. That really hurt him.

To a mother, the worst thing you can ever do is hurt her child. Although at first, I tried to see things with an open mind, I understand Corbin feeling like an outsider. It should come as little surprise that there was a lot of bad blood brewing at the time of the accident.

When we were first thrown into this nightmare none of that entered my mind. We put all of the differences aside, and Jeff and I got back on the horse taking over as Corbin's parents. We discussed what was best for him and the other kids at that time. We spent a lot of time alone with Corbin, met with doctors, and discussed the future we all might face once he left the hospital. There were days that Jeff, Angie, Steve, and I sat together in Corbin's room with no issues between us.

Angie supported Jeff just like Steve supported me. The petty feuds that often littered our relationship weren't the priority, so it was all put aside. Nothing mattered but healing Corbin. That harmony was short-lived however, as the issues that existed between us could only be held at bay for so long.

Boring Day - Journal Entry — July 14, 2018

Corb was pretty stable all night. He still has a fever, but he's on a few different antibiotics for infection. His vitals and the pressure in his head were all where they wanted them to be, and the plan remained the same to keep him resting and healing. The nurse noticed Corbin's right foot was very swollen, warm, and red this morning. So, they called for an Ultrasound. They wanted to look at his belly where surgery was as well as for clots on the right side of his body where the femoral artery catheter was inserted at Concord Hospital. Apparently, these spots are problem areas for causing clots.

They encourage us to leave (aka kick us out) on these slow, low agenda days. We all left for a few hours to get some fresh air. Jeff got back before me and went up to see Corbin. I was in the lobby visiting with family when Jeff called, and he told me that I needed to come to the room right then. No information except to come right away. Turns out they were worried that he was having a seizure. The swollen right leg was badly shaking. Neurology rushed in and determined that it was reflexes where his body loses control with a brain injury.

During this scare, the ultrasound team was in the room and explained that they found a pocket of fluid in his abdomen where his spleen used to be which they aren't worried about. However, they are concerned about a small clot near the PICC line and an aneurysm near where the femoral line was. The first course of action is an extended ultrasound with pressure to fix the aneurysm, which is what they were doing when the leg started shaking. The clot is small enough that they can fix it with medication, but the aneurysm is large. The ultrasound pressure was ineffective, so the plan is to go in with a needle and try to clot it tomorrow.

The thought of an aneurysm was petrifying. They were hereditary in Jeff's family, and I knew the damage they could do after Jeff's father had one burst many years before. It was the same leg that's swollen, so I knew it could potentially cut off blood flow and perhaps lead to amputation. The challenges were just never ending.

Leaving was difficult enough but to leave and come back to a scare like this made it much more difficult. It makes you appreciate what you used to take for granted. I would have killed for a boring day sitting around the house doing nothing or even tending bar. I went into a daydream and envisioned a normal summer day with no plans and nowhere to go. Just time with the kids at home playing in the water, music blasting, grilling dinner, and soaking up the sun. I didn't appreciate those days enough when they were commonplace and now, I was begging for just one.

I glanced up at the calendar that hung in Corbin's room and noted the ten crossed out days since Corbin arrived. Today was July 14th and I've felt the sun on my skin no more than three days over the last few weeks. I kept telling myself we'll get there, and I'll never take it for granted again.

10

HE JUST MIGHT BE THAT KID

By this point, things were getting difficult with the other kids. Grayson was with Steve's family, and they would bring him a few times a week to see us. Grace had Mari there with her still, and they were staying next door at the hotel with my mom as well as Tanna. Cohen was staying with Jeff and Angie at a hotel, and he would spend his days at the hospital with the rest of us. This was such uncharted territory for me as a Mom.

I had no idea how to parent the other kids as all my focus was on Corbin. I've heard that this is what it is like to have children born with disabilities. The parent spends all of their time focused on the less abled child and the able-bodied offspring gets ignored. That's what this seemed like to me. Visitation schedules were out the window, work was out the window, life as any of us knew it was out the window. I know that I needed to spend time with the other kids too, but it's entirely possible that I have the rest of my life with them. I may only have minutes or days with Corbin.

I felt the worst for Cohen. He was spending his summer vacation in a hospital sitting in waiting rooms or watching his big brother cling to life. No friends and no fun. Reluctantly but with good cause, we left for the afternoon to watch our beloved Red Sox. Just Steve, Cohen, and me, and it was great. The hospital was within walking distance from Fenway Park, and it was a beautiful day. Leave it to Steve's mom to get us great seats for the Sox against the Toronto Blue Jays game.

About halfway through the game, someone from the Red Sox organization came up and tapped me on the shoulder. He asked if we were Corbin's family. I told him we were. He said that our family was in their thoughts, and he handed us a huge bag of Red Sox gear. I'm sure this was Brenda working her magic again, and it was another reason why I hated to lose her when Steve and I officially parted ways. She always has a way of going above and beyond.

Not long after the accident, she reached out to Julian Edelman, the star wide receiver for the Patriots, and told him about Corbin's accident. Edelman was Corbin's favorite player in any sport. Within days a package arrived with a handwritten get-well card, a signed hat, and Edelman's book. It was incredible. I knew if and when Corbin could see it, he would lose his mind. Brenda knew that he would love this, and it was something we can tell him about; it was a gesture to spark something, anything to get him to come back.

The hospital isn't an easy place to be, never mind living in the ICU. When we were in the room with the glass doors, we had to have the curtains closed most of the time. We were very isolated from the outside world, as were the other rooms. Many of the rooms had posters on the glass showing the children when they were healthy and happy. It made me wonder what was wrong with each patient. We couldn't see them on the other side of the curtain, and we had no idea if they were in as bad a shape as Corbin.

By now we started to recognize the familiar faces of the parents when we were in the waiting room to visit family or passing in the hall. They all looked very similar to how I felt. Blank stares, no sleep, lacking a good warm shower, and slowly dying inside. That night when I went down to get my tea, a woman struck up a conversation with me. She was a nurse who lived in Florida. Her nephew was in his early twenties and had a terrible diagnosis. She was up visiting to try to give some relief to his parents.

We talked, told the stories of the kids, and cried. We soon realized that we'd taken longer away than planned and decided to go back up. I was going to the seventh floor, while she was going to the ninth. We hugged and said goodbye, reassuring the other that we'd keep each other and our boys in our thoughts.

I walked in still thinking about the pleasant conversation while a bit unnerved about how long I had been away. As luck would have it, I was in for quite a shock when I returned. I was staying in the room alone at that point because Steve had to go back to work. I walked into the room and noticed a nurse I wasn't familiar with. She was very animated and eager to share some incredible news with me. Corbin had opened his eyes while I was downstairs gabbing. Though they were closed again now, the nurse had seen it happen and that was good enough for me.

How does that happen? I'm with this kid around the clock for weeks, and he waits until I leave to come back to life? Seems like a cruel joke, but at the same time, I couldn't be happier. I wanted nothing more than to see some life in him, to look in his eyes, to see my son alive on the inside. All along, my gut told me he was in there. I felt like if I could look in his eyes, then I'd know for sure.

He did it once, and he'll do it again. Nothing was going to take that pure happiness away. I was so proud of him. He was fighting to come back with all the strength he could muster. It gave me a huge dose of strength and reassurance that my Corbin was there.

Slow and Steady - Journal Entry — July 16, 2018

After last night, I couldn't bring myself to leave Corbin's side fearing that I would miss something. His nurse reassured me if there was any action, she would wake me up. The rest of the night was uneventful, but he responded to me in a big way this morning. I can only describe it as the feeling you get holding your baby for the first time. He's still my baby, and less than two weeks ago we were told to say goodbye. To have him show any semblance of life and press his face against mine, when I thought I might never have that again, is indescribable.

We live hour to hour here, and these small glimmers of hope keep us going. The rest of the day was pretty calm. A new drain was placed in his stomach to empty the pocket of fluid where his spleen was, and they tried to repair the aneurysm. We were told by his nurse that it was successful but should have the full report tomorrow. His other limbs will also get an ultrasound tomorrow to check for clots. So far, the only other thing on the agenda is to clamp the drain in his head to see if they can stop draining the fluid from his skull as his body may do it on its own. It's just one baby step at a time.

11

STUFF'S ABOUT TO HIT THE FAN

So, everything was feeling positive with Corbin's progress. That should have been the only thing we cared about, but the tension was starting to build elsewhere. Ill feelings were brewing between my family and Angie way before this, and even though I was still playing nice, she was starting to step on toes. I accept the fact that it is difficult being the new contestant in a game of Family Feud, but things were starting to get tense when my family was there to visit.

On one occasion, Jeff and I were having a conversation about the fundraising efforts and how we needed to use the money wisely. We decided to open a bank account for all donations so we could make accommodations to the house when he got home. We didn't know exactly what we would need, be it a lift, ramps, a special shower, or medical equipment. We had no idea how much he was going to need, or how much it was going to cost. Though, we agreed that the best thing was a joint account in both our names.

After that, I learned that Jeff went home, and it was decided that the funds would be split between the two of us. I screamed, "Absolutely not. The money isn't for us. The money is for Corbin's needs."

Corbin lived with me full time, and it was our house that was going to need to have the accommodations. Within days, Angie's sister set up a bank account without either Jeff's or my name on it, and they wanted all the money raised for Corbin to be put in that account. As you can imagine, that wasn't going to fly.

Angie would argue with me about not getting the free parking pass or asking me to split a Subway gift card that was donated. All in all, the sh*t was about to hit the proverbial fan. With everything else that we had to deal with, this was really an unnecessary addition to the pile of stress we were all trying to escape.

We had a "family meeting" scheduled for Corbin's doctors to meet with the parents to go over the plans of care and future prognosis. Decisions would need to be made by the parents on different treatments as well. I told Jeff that I did not want her in the meeting. We are Corbin's parents, not Steve and not Angie. I insisted that we were the only two involved in these decisions, and if he didn't agree then the current friendly arrangements would change.

For a short time longer, Jeff, Angie, and I remained cordial when in Corbin's room at the same time. I was a permanent fixture in the room, and Grace started staying in there with me once Steve left to go back to work. Jeff and Angie were still staying in hotels with Cohen and their daughter Keira. On most days, Jeff would get there before Angie and the kids would come over, but once they all got there it got a little tight in Corbin's room. Cohen and Keira sat on the back window seat together and played on cell phones.

It was no way for these kids to be spending their summer, but circumstances dictated that sitting and texting were going to be their primary activities. Grace and I would frequently take Cohen and Keira to get lunch once Jeff and Angie were both there. We would take Keira down to the cafeteria for food or up to play in the outdoor garden on the top floor of the hospital. To anyone who didn't know the dynamics of what was bubbling beneath the surface, it seemed to be the perfect co-parenting situation. Things are rarely as they seem to the outside. Our nerves were wearing thin and toes were getting stepped on.

Never a Dull Moment - Journal Entry – July 17, 2018

Corbin has two devices in his skull. One is called a "bolt" that was put in at Concord Hospital, and it monitors the pressure in his skull caused by the brain swelling and fluid that's building up. The other device measures those things, but it also has a drain on it so when that pressure gets too high, they can open it up and drain the fluid to drop the pressure. A fairly good amount of fluid is drained every day.

The neurosurgeons would like to take these devices out so they can do an MRI and try to wake him up again. Today was the test. The drain was clamped in hopes that his body would get rid of the fluid on its own, like the rest of our bodies do. If he can do that for twenty-four hours while the drain is clamped, then they will take the bolt out on Wednesday. By the way, I've been promised an honorary MD before we get out of here, and I think I've earned it.

Corbin has had little spikes with stimulation, but as long as they don't last long, they're happy. He has done pretty well all day, but he has gotten more sensitive as the day progresses. By the end of the night, if I started talking to him or even trying to hold his hand, his ICP would spike. So, we've kept the room quiet and dark all day. Around 11 p.m., I was whispering with his two nurses about things they're watching for and the plan for the next few hours.

I began thinking, well this is kind of going to be a boring post tonight. All of a sudden, one nurse notices something unusual. It looks like he's trying to cough or take deep breaths even though he's still on a breathing tube. His deep breaths become eyes wide open, full blinking, and then his body shakes like he's freezing cold. I rushed up to try to relax him, tell him that I'm there, and that he is all right.

At the same time, the nurses rushed to give him sedation because his ICP spiked to the mid-forties. His breathing machine showed him triggering breaths, meaning that he was trying to breathe on his own. OMG, I JUST SAW HIM WAKE UP FOR ABOUT twenty SECONDS. It was terrifying and incredible at the same time.

The hope is that this is happening because the brain swelling has gone down enough that his body is not only getting rid of the fluid like it's supposed to, but he's becoming more aware. He's still on an incredible amount of pain medication and sedation so this was pretty shocking. That was such an adrenaline rush that I'm more tired than usual.

I was nearing mid-semester of a crash course in ICU medicine. Besides being in the room and asking for an explanation for everything that was done to Corbin, every medicine given, viewing X-rays and MRI images, I also attended rounds at the change of shifts twice a day. The nurses and doctors taking over for the day would meet outside the patients' rooms and discuss what had occurred during the last twelve hours. This was followed by the plan of action for the upcoming day.

Once I was briefed by Dr. Mooney, we would go out to the hall and join the rest of Corbin's medical team for the day. They all listened to me like I was one of the team. They allowed me to speak and give my opinion, and often they would try to accommodate my ideas into their plan. It gave a mom who felt so helpless a sense of purpose, like I was having some part in taking care of him and making him well.

The drains in Corbin's head had been in much longer than they hoped they would be. They were a huge infection risk being in that long, and the medical team began to question how effective they are reading after that long a time. Getting them removed was becoming a priority. It was a scary thought for me to have them removed. I had watched those pressure numbers diligently since day one and seeing them reassured me his brain wasn't swelling much. Not having them in meant that it was a guessing game. The swelling in his brain by normal standards would have peaked in the first seventy-two hours, and here we are almost two weeks later and it's still spiking.

Doctors explained that clamping the drain was the first step. They did this and needed to see if Corbin's body could get rid of the fluid on its own. We watched tensely after they clamped it, and we were thrilled that it was working. His body was successfully trying to manage the pressure on its own, but any bit of stimulation affected him. I sat quietly by his side watching those numbers all day praying for them to stay normal.

Any movement from Corbin was initially scary, and then it became thrilling. My initial thought when I'd see him move was, *Oh My God. What's wrong? Is he okay?* Then it became, *Oh My God. It's Corbin. He's trying to wake up.* I'd watch him, unsure of what was really happening. The dark cloud of doubt would set in, and I'd wonder if his movements were just a reflex.

No one knew if the Corbin we had before the accident was still in there. We didn't know how bad the damage was. We didn't even know if Corbin would ever wake up again. So, any sign of life from Corbin was terrifying. Was it going to show us what we had been praying for or what we were dreading? Either way, when I saw his eyes open and then he took breaths on his own, it felt like a miracle.

12

HALF A GOOF IS BETTER
THAN NONE

*T*wo Weeks - Journal Entry — July 18, 2018

  I can't believe it's been two weeks. You become conditioned in only two weeks to the things you see and hear. I should have kept track of the number of different doctors I've spoken to, the number of consent forms I've signed, and the number of nurses Corbin's had. In just two weeks, I think Corbin has had twelve surgical procedures. That's one tough kid!

  He has always been a procrastinator, and this is no different. He's doing it all on his time. The neurosurgeons and neurologists want to push him, but he's taking his sweet time. I tell him every day to take as much time as he needs. Corbin has had the drain in his head clamped for about thirty-six hours, and he is handling it very well. They haven't had to open it, even once, which is what they hoped for. This indicates that his body is figuring out how to get rid of the fluid on its own.

He also had the "bolt" taken out of his head today. That was crazy to watch. It was unscrewed from his skull like an auto mechanic changing a carburetor. He keeps trying to cough on his own and then opens his eyes. It's so great to see life in him. His arms are loosely restrained because they say teenagers can be unpredictable when they wake up. They can't risk him pulling the breathing tube out.

At this point, they aren't even trying to wake him. He's still heavily sedated, but they think the swelling in his brain has gone down and he's becoming more aware. He is likely building a tolerance to all of the medications, and that could be why he's trying to wake up. So, we continue to take baby steps in the right direction.

The longest two weeks of my life came to an end, and yet I knew this was just the start. The doctors at Children's warned us that we could be in the hospital for up to six months. We weren't in a sprint to the finish. This was a marathon and finishing the race was the only option. More than just your typical 26.2 miles however, this was a marathon run blindfolded in the dark where you were constantly scared of what you may run into next or if you were about to walk off a cliff.

It was hard to get comfortable with the acceptance that he was improving because the reality was, he could fall off a cliff at any second. I would keep telling myself that he's going to be okay. I had to continue to focus on the right now, not the tonight or even tomorrow. Right now, he's here and he's alive.

While gazing at his resting face, I thought back to the day that Corbin gave us our first scare when he was about two and a half, not long after Grace was born. We had big dogs. Corbin had gotten out of the tub and felt he needed to let the dogs out. I was still in the bathroom getting Grace out of the tub when I heard a scream. He had opened the front door of the house and got knocked down the stairs by the dogs.

The landing was stone, and he was bleeding badly from his head. Luckily, Paul was on the rescue squad and came right over. They determined he needed stitches, so we took our first Corbin ambulance ride. They put me on the stretcher with Corbin on my lap, and off to the hospital we went to get his forehead stitched up.

Later that fall, my friend Lisa came over, with her children who were close to the same age as Corbin and Grace. We were going to bring them all out to play. Lisa went out with her daughter and the two boys while I got Grace dressed. They were out there for less than five minutes without me. We had a six-month-old lab puppy that the boys were chasing around. When I came out, I didn't see the boys, so I called for them. Only her son, Colby, popped up from behind the dirt pile they were playing on. Both Corbin and the puppy were gone.

The police got involved and shut down the nearby gravel pit as they feared he might have wandered there. We had neighbors on four-wheelers searching the woods as we lived on twenty-seven acres in the woods, and he could have been anywhere. I don't know how many barefoot miles I ran that day through the woods. He was missing for almost two hours before I heard someone scream my name saying they found him.

I fell to the ground and started crying. He and the dog were found at the transfer station. Luckily, someone was there that day burning brush when all of a sudden, they saw a puppy and a little boy following close behind. That one took a few years off my life.

Grace was my full-time bunk buddy. She would sleep in the recliner right beside my little window bed. Grace and Corbin were twenty-one months apart and the best of friends since they were tiny. This was devastating for her. She would sit by his side and lay her head by his arm. She felt as helpless as he did in some ways. They were kindred spirits. We all tried to find our little ways of doing what we could to feel like we were helping.

Grace came up with the idea of the bracelets to sell to raise money and awareness. She helped design them by making them Corbin's favorite color and made sure the green ribbon for brain injury awareness was included in the design. We went to the store together so she could get his favorite color string, and she made him a bracelet of his own. Even though he was restrained and there were tubes and lines everywhere, the nurses let her loosely tie it on his wrist so something from her was with him at all times.

Before the accident occurred, Grace had been begging to go to a special field hockey camp at the Dartmouth College campus. Field hockey was the only sport Grace played, and she absolutely loved it. She really wanted to improve her skills for the upcoming season, so I made sure it happened. The date to leave was fast approaching and Grace refused to leave Corbin. I reminded her that she was fifteen, it was summer vacation, and how much she was looking forward to it. She needed the break.

I assured her that I would update her multiple times a day, and she could call and text any time she wanted. The camp was only for four days. Although, I understood her feelings, I wanted her to go. In Grace's mind, nothing was more important than being there for Corbin. Ultimately, Mom prevailed, and Grace was off to enjoy at least part of her summer.

Jeff drove her up, and she texted the entire time she was there, checking in on her brother. She wasn't perfectly convinced that she should be there, but she promised to make the best of it.

My Dreaded Day - Journal Entry — July 20, 2018

So, as many times as I've been told they want an MRI ASAP, and yet, I'm told there's no rush because it doesn't change the course of action. I'm personally in no rush. Do I want to know what Corbin's capabilities will be? Of course, but from my experience with neurologists, some seem to make judgments too quickly and they are on the negative end, to put it lightly. We have grieved losing Corbin way too many times in the last two weeks. An MRI will show the extent of the damage in much more detail.

I've tried to keep these posts about Corbin's recovery, not about how I'm holding up, or how it's affecting his siblings, or the hundreds of other things it's impacting. But today that's harder to do. His first MRI is scheduled for today. I feel like it's the day before the accident and I know it's going to happen, but I can't stop it. I've had a good handle on all of it until now. I'm petrified about what they are going to tell us. It's hard to get the negative prognosis out of my mind.

Don't get me wrong we have lots of hope, and no matter what they say we will continue to fight right beside Corbin for the rest of his life. We will get him every tool possible to get him better. He has to have a few things done first, like all the staples removed from his abdomen. They have to lay him flat and make sure he can handle it. There isn't a scheduled time for the MRI, so we have no idea when it will be.

It will just be a day full of scary anticipation. On day one we were all outside of the OR waiting to see if he would even survive the surgery. When they came out and told us they would be wheeling him by. I looked at Corbin's Auntie, Christine, and said, "That means he's alive!" And she said, "Yup and we can deal with the rest." As long as he's here with us then we can handle the rest. I go back to that often, and I'm trying to think that way today.

The trauma doctor also told me not to focus on what the MRI says, *what matters is what Corbin shows us. The MRI will also show us a clearer picture of his spinal cord and if any of the fractures in his spine have damaged it. So, whether you believe in prayer or positive thoughts and energy, today would be the day for extra of each.*

I wasn't sure that I could handle the results of the MRI. I feared the worse and how could I not? I can't count the number of times I had seen the basic reflex tests which resulted in the smallest amount of brain activity, followed by the look on the face of the neurologist when they didn't see the results they hoped to see. At this point their facial expressions were likely a mix of fear and sadness, while mine was a look of disgust and disbelief. I would repeatedly think to myself, *You don't know him! I know my son. You don't know how sensitive he is to medications.* I'm sure it was merely denial to protect myself but, at the time, I fully believed it.

I almost didn't want to know, and yet, I wanted nothing more to do with guessing how bad his brain was damaged. God, I wanted to be positive. However, besides that machines were still keeping him alive, and a few times opening his eyes over the two weeks after the accident, there were a lot more unknowns and negative probabilities surrounding us.

If they come back and tell me that he's going to be bedridden for life with no communication ability, then I'll get the house ready to accommodate his needs and take him home. If he has to be in rehab for years to come, we'll move from New Hampshire and be by his side every step of the way. I will take him and take care of him no matter what condition he's in. Any of those scenarios were better than not having him at all.

Here We Go . . . Journal Entry — July 20, 2018

Corb got the staples taken out of his stomach at 9 a.m. and then began the test of lying flat. He handled both with no issues. By 11 a.m. they had him all packaged up, and a team was here to move him. He was gone for four hours. Lots of images were needed. When we were allowed back in the room, they said he did great. No crazy spikes in vitals or any other issues.

One of the neurosurgeons come in pretty quickly and said from their viewpoint, no brain surgeries were needed. Great? I honestly had never been told that might be something they were looking for but good news, I guess. He did tell us that they saw damage to the brain stem and the basal ganglia parts of the brain. He said it was not really his department and that neurology would explain more.

We had already been told that with bad enough damage to the brain stem it would lead to death. So, I instantly turned to google and found a test that's performed to figure that out. Corbin is doing every single thing except for one mentioned in the test. The one he's not doing is breathing on his own and that's because he's on a machine. He is constantly triggering the machine trying to breathe on his own, and he was breathing on his own before they sedated him so heavily.

Shortly after that, neurosurgeon #2 came in and explained that there were multiple spots of damage in his brain and at this point, they can't tell us what functions he will or won't have. He said it's like a bunch of light switches, and we need Corbin to show us which ones still work. Once again, he's in surgery so we need to wait for neurology to come in to give us a clear explanation.

The night continued and no one else came in, not neurology and not the ortho doctors to explain if there was damage to his spinal cord with all the fractures he has. The second surgeon said he didn't believe there was damage to the spinal cord, but we would have to wait for that department to let us know for sure.

So, we begin the here we go, let's hurry up and wait, yet again. Corbin's morphine has been dropped daily for the last three days and being on it as long as he has, he will have withdrawals. So, at this time, they are reducing one medication at a time. Not both in conjunction like last time. It will be easier to treat the withdrawals that way. Once the morphine is low enough, the sedation will come down slowly also.

After dreading this day so much, I've decided it doesn't matter what the neurologists say. I know what I've seen, I know what I feel, and I know Corbin. They can look at these tests and come up with all the prognoses they want. I'm sure they will come in tomorrow and have doom and gloom to report to us. I will get upset, but my child is still alive. He can take all the time he needs, and we will give him every tool there is to heal him. We will never give up on him.

They have this saying I learned about during our time at Children's called the "July Effect." Every July, the hospitals get a new batch of first-year medical residents in. Corbin had his upper-level team that oversaw everything, but during the day there was a resident that oversaw his care. Corbin's resident was a woman, and on more than one occasion I could feel her lack of confidence and it worried me. I would second guess her or ask for her assessment to be run by the supervising doctors before she made any decisions on Corbin.

This morning she told me Corbin needed the staples removed that were closing his abdomen before he could go in for the MRI. Dr. Mooney was going to be gone for the next few days, but we had gone over everything before he left. One of the topics we discussed was that he didn't need his staples out for the MRI. Once again, I stopped the resident and told her what Dr. Mooney had told me. She seemed unsure and left the room.

When she came back, she told me that they had been in long enough, and it was time to have them out. She then proceeded to ask me if she could. Can you? Why is a doctor asking me? *I don't know doctor, can you?* I thought to myself. Well that didn't sit well with me, and I told her that I didn't want her touching him. Rosa was on a break, and I wasn't having anything done to him without her there to tell me it was okay. I trusted Rosa, who had been doing this for years, over the resident who just started.

When Rosa returned, I explained what happened. I told her that I felt bad, but it very much came across like the resident didn't know what she was doing. Rosa left and had a talk with her. The resident came in and explained that she did know what she was doing and apologized for the way she presented herself. All was well, we agreed to have the staples removed, while Rosa and I supervised very closely.

All of the focus has been on Corbin's brain when the fact was, we didn't even know if Corbin might be paralyzed. This MRI was supposed to give us lots of answers to more than just his brain. The X-rays showed multiple spinal fractures, but we had no idea how his spinal cord may have come through the crash. From the preliminary X-rays it looked promising. Imagine spinal cord damage and paralysis being an afterthought. If his brain doesn't work, the rest really doesn't matter.

From the start, we knew the brain stem being too badly damaged was the worst-case scenario, so to hear that they could visibly see damage to it was awful news. The brain stem sends messages from the brain to the rest of the body. It controls basic functions like breathing, swallowing, heart rate, and blood pressure.

Severe damage to it can cause someone to be in a vegetative state or even death. Well, Corbin was still alive and was showing some signs of alertness that you don't get when in a vegetative state, but the doctors were convinced we were not out of the woods with that.

Dropping his pain medication and consequently, his level of sedation, was scary. It had gone badly the first time, but they were taking a new route which made much more sense to me. Corbin had shown from the beginning how sensitive he was to change. Rosa spoke to me about how the medications he was on were very strong, and he would go through the same kind of withdrawals a drug user would. Vomiting, fluctuating body temperature, agitation, the chance of seizures.

The hits keep coming. This poor kid has been through so much. He's not even awake and now this is what he has to go through. How much can one body stand to go through? All I could do was stay close by and watch every number on the machines, watch and listen for any change or distress, keep reassuring him to fight, and tell him how proud I was and how much I loved him for the nine-millionth time.

That's a Win - Journal Entry — July 21, 2018

It's so hard to convey the severity of Corbin's condition. I might talk about an MRI one day, but a hundred other issues are still lingering. All day long, teams of doctors from departments I didn't even know existed in the medical world come into Corbin's room. It's like a revolving door. He has so many issues that I would need pages upon pages every night if I talked about each thing, we get thrown at us during the day. I try to limit it to the major issues each day.

I've been asked a few times by family if they can post some pictures of Corbin in the hospital, and I have been pretty adamant that no one does. I am still a private person and obviously very protective of Corbin. I don't want anyone seeing him like this. However, I've started to realize that these pictures might help show the reality of our lives and the reality of what we as his parents are trying to comprehend. Also, what his siblings and family are trying to accept and process.

Which brings me to our meeting with neurology today. I will try to give the short version. The best news was that they do not believe there was any damage to his spinal cord. As far as his brain, they see very widespread damage. Damage to the white matter and gray matter. They believe that the most damaged areas will affect cognition and physical motor skills. He could wake up like a newborn and might not be able to control his limbs. He did say there is hope.

He said like everyone else has, we need to see what Corbin shows us, and what he shows us, in the beginning, isn't the end result. The rehab team that works with both Boston Children's and Spaulding Rehabilitation Hospital is going to start meeting with him right away to track his progress to learn what they can to give Corbin the best possible recovery. They told us that he will be going to Spaulding at some point whenever he is well enough to leave Children's. We have all done our research. Spaulding is where we wanted him to go for rehab, so we were very happy they agreed that was the place for Corbin.

So, we're pretty much guaranteed that the Corbin we said goodbye to on the morning of July 4th won't be the Corbin that wakes up, but as we hoped, Corbin is still here. We get to kiss Corbin and tell him that we love him every day. Most importantly, Corbin is still fighting and has already defied so many odds. That's a win in my book.

13

I'M TRYING AND I'M STILL HERE

C orbin is a genuine miracle. I want to take a moment to recap the little miracles along the way, which when added together, equal one huge miracle. Miracle number one was that he was wearing his seat belt, and it was one of the primary reasons he is here today. When all of this is over, no matter the end result, I will be a seat belt advocate.

Miracle number two occurred when we learned from our local Boscawen Police Department that Corbin's cousin Tanna, who was in the back seat with him during the accident, could have crawled out of the car like the two kids in the front seat did. He knew Corbin was unconscious though, and he thought he heard Corbin choking. He made the bold and brave decision to remain in the car and held Corbin's head upright until paramedics got there and cut the roof off of the car to get to Corbin. This kept his airway open and allowed oxygen to continue to Corbin's brain. Without his quick thinking, compassion, and heroics, the ending of this story would have been very different.

We live in a small town with a volunteer medical team and fire department. When they arrived on the crash scene and realized how severe Corbin's injuries were, they called Concord, a much larger department. As a result, he was transported to the hospital by their team. During that fifteen-mile ride to the hospital they almost lost him, and they had to call for a second ambulance to bring more supplies on the way.

He survived the first surgery despite losing more than half his blood supply, a fractured spine, broken bones, having organs removed, brain damage, and an incision in his abdomen as long as his arm. Corbin's cousin Paul was one of the first people there with me. With all of his experience in a Level 1 trauma center, he was calm, cool, collected and asked all the right questions. His knowledge and willingness to take control of the situation played a huge part in the care that Corbin ultimately received.

Once we learned that there was a room at Children's, we learned there were no aircrafts in the area of New Hampshire, Maine, or Massachusetts. They began looking to Connecticut but with the severity of Corbin's condition, they decided to divert one from Worcester, Massachusetts, to come and get to him. Once on the helicopter they almost lost him again. He was given more blood and rushed into surgery with just an over the phone consent from me because there was no other choice if we're going to save him.

Working through all the miraculous details of his survival, it is clear to see a recurring pattern. This kid is defying the odds, and it's as if all the stars have lined up in perfect harmony to ensure his likely survival. He should have been dead several times but much like the proverbial cat with nine lives, it's not meant to be. Though he was using them up mighty quickly, his time isn't now. I didn't care what else they told me, or what test results they came back with. I knew he was meant for more and death was not in his immediate future.

I never stop being in awe of the love and support we are getting from what seems like half the world. Our families have been absolute lifesavers. My mom spends much of the week at home taking over my visitation schedule with Cohen and comes down here to be with us the other part of the week. Paul, our lifesaver from day one, is with me almost every single day. He answers questions I have and knows the questions to ask that I wouldn't have a clue about.

He always has a positive attitude and is the first to get Corbin anything he needs. I've enjoyed his company so much through this. My cousin Jenn is taking care of my house and animals. She tried really hard to keep the garden and flowers going, but apparently, it's a pretty hot, dry summer. I assured her that it was the least of my concerns and to please not stress about it. She visits multiple times a week, brings me cards and gifts from people in town, and just wants to be there for me in every way.

On top of all that, Jenn and Aunt Jan are working hard every day, ordering gear that they can sell to raise money for Corbin's care, or trying to plan fundraising events to help in every way they can. Brenda, Steve's mom has a flexible schedule as a real estate agent and has completely taken over my role with Grayson. She is taking care of him while Steve's at work and I'm at the hospital. She brings him to see me a few times a week, which is both heartwarming and heartbreaking. Grayson doesn't understand why he can't stay with mom.

The rest of our family checks in daily with encouraging love and support. The support is from all over the world. People in France bought Corbin's bracelets, people in Pakistan sent in pictures wearing Corbin strong T-shirts, and the following on the CaringBridge page is in the tens of thousands and growing daily. The comments and stories people leave after a post lifts my spirits and brings me to tears. I read them all to Corbin daily. People send us meals, gas cards, and continue to care for our homes, animals, and children. It is so incredible and though I allude to it often, we wouldn't be where we are without this support.

The Calm Before the Storm? Journal Entry — July 22, 2018

It's strangely calm in his room. He doesn't spike his vitals much anymore, and they have dropped his morphine as low as they're going to go for now. They did start to lower the sedation tonight. So, we're going to wait and see how long it's going to take for all of these drugs to get out of his system. Wait to see if he's going to have withdrawals and, most importantly, wait to see him wake up and show us what he's capable of.

We've been warned about what we might see with withdrawals and the medications like methadone he might have to be put on. They say he could be combative, and it's often scary to watch. It can't be scarier than what we've already been through. I'll take seeing him react over lying lifeless any day. Corbin has made a few improvements in the last few days. He would be so mad that I am announcing this, but he doesn't need to be straight cathed every four hours anymore. He's urinating on his own! His bowels are finally working also, so those are both very important.

He is also moving his eyes away from the light when they check his pupils. He's very often triggering his breathing machine and trying to breathe on his own. I lightly massage his scalp and he scrunches his shoulders and twitches. It reminds me of a puppy when you find that spot to scratch, and they can't control that back leg from kicking. It's sweet to have him respond to our touch.

Tomorrow he will be sent down to radiology to have a feeding tube placed down through his nose. Typically, they do it right in his room, and they have tried twice, but he has so many facial fractures that they can't get it to pass. So, X-rays will be used. They will also check the aneurysm they worked on last week to make sure it's healing the way they want. Besides that, we wait.

It feels like the calm before the storm. It hasn't been this quiet and calm in his room this entire time, and we know it could all go in any direction once he wakes up. So, we are trying to rest up and enjoy our quiet time with him before the next leg of this journey starts.

Calm of course is always a relative term. There are still countless teams tending to and monitoring everything in and out of the room all day. We received some positives about his spine and his body functions working on their own. Positive unless you are the poor nurse who has to change the bed when the bodily functions began functioning of course. You look for the tiniest rays of hope, and it keeps you from giving up.

We will soon be asked to attend a very scary meeting though. Along with the good always came the bad. His morphine was low enough and sedation was being lowered, but they still aren't seeing what they believed they should. This means the idea of him waking up is getting slimmer. We have been told what we were seeing, with his eyes opening and the small body movements, could be all he ever does. I refused to let that thought get in my head though. I wasn't going to allow that to be it. The meeting has been scheduled to discuss this.

As if there isn't enough chaos going on each day with Corbin, tensions are still running high between Jeff, Angie, and me. One would think amid the challenges we are faced with, that adults wouldn't act like children, but that isn't the case. It has become a bit of a circus sideshow taking place outside the center ring. With the meeting coming up with the medical team, I put my foot down and I made sure that it was Jeff and me only. I really wanted Paul in the meeting with us too. He had a way of keeping the emotions that Jeff and I were feeling out of it while asking the important questions we might not think to.

I knew banning Angie from the meeting would mean they would ban Paul in return. Paul is Jeff's cousin and Jeff knew his value, but he wouldn't cross his wife for anyone. Even though I was talking with Jeff I was never actually dealing directly with Jeff. I was quite aware that nothing was truly Jeff's decision, and I wasn't going to allow that when it came to Corbin's medical care.

I met with the social worker and asked about my rights, and as I suspected I had all the right to keep decisions made to Jeff and me. Also, as I suspected, by me doing that, Jeff wasn't going to allow me to bring Paul in. All I wanted to do was concentrate on Corbin. This extra drama was so unnecessary but not at all unexpected.

Corbin Strong - Journal Entry — July 24, 2018

Hopefully, no one worried too much with no post to wake up to early this morning. I was just too exhausted last night. I wanted to talk about how amazing everyone at Boston Children's Hospital is. Corbin's nurse Rosa hung a banner in his room and one of his other regular nurses, Jay, showed up the other night with a container of chocolate chip cookies that his wife and boys made for us. They feel like family, and they truly care about all of us. They are protective of Corbin and are always making sure that he is getting everything he needs. It's so incredible. It feels like we're getting special treatment, but they swear it's their goal to make sure everyone feels that way.

Yesterday was somewhat uneventful. He did have a feeding tube put in, so he's getting small amounts for food now which is great. The spinal surgeon came in and told us that his MRI actually looked better than he expected it to. He went over all the fractures in his spine and some in the back of his rib cage that we didn't actually even know about. He believes they will all heal on their own without surgery. He will have to leave the neck brace on for at least six weeks because ligaments were pulled, and it helps the bones heal correctly. We'll take it!

The aneurysm isn't completely fixed so they will work on that again this week. Besides that, we sit and wait for the sedation to be low enough and see how he responds. Jeff and I have a meeting with a bunch of the teams of doctors later today. They will talk about different scenarios that we could face when the sedation is off, and what levels of consciousness he could or couldn't be in, in addition to what the plan would be for each of them. So that's a little stressful, but I'm still holding onto letting Corbin show me.

Perhaps, the highlight of what was sure to be a very stressful day was the fact that Corbin got his hair washed. Anyone who had been in the room knows how badly he needed it, and how much it made me crazy. I brushed it every day and could never get all the dried blood and debris out without soap and water so that was very exciting for me. I constantly groom and moisturize him.

As expected, our family meeting day was beyond stressful. We had no idea what we would hear, as we were finally going to have all of Corbin's teams of doctors in one room at the same time. They would have all of the test results with them, and all of them would be at our disposal to answer any questions we had after they spoke. I don't think I could have actually prepared myself for what they were going to say. I also worried about what was going to happen when the social worker told Jeff and Angie that Angie was not going to be able to attend the meeting. The tension was running high, to say the least.

Despite the negative cloud hanging over the room, we had a lot to be thankful for. Corbin's medical team was becoming like family to us. They cared for us and protected us completely. Corbin's room was decorated with pictures and things Corbin would love. For Rosa to have that big red banner made was so thoughtful and sweet. She will always be a part of our lives.

We were called to the meeting room once all of the doctors had gathered. Jeff and I followed the nurse silently down the hall with no eye contact and no words. The tension could've been cut with a knife. I knew he wasn't happy with me and not allowing Angie in the meeting was going to cause trouble for him. My concern was Corbin though, and everyone else came second.

The meeting itself was shattering. The doctors told us that he should be doing more, and they don't have confidence that he will ever wake up. He also doesn't qualify for rehab at a facility like Spaulding so they would set up some tours for us at long term care facilities. I listened to each one spew more negative news, and I could feel my stomach tie itself into knots and my blood begin to boil. They all took turns providing their version of reality. It all came down to the fact that there was not enough brain activity.

"What do you mean?" I asked as tears rolled down my face. "You told us previously that Spaulding was the place for him!"

They explained that was what they initially hoped but Corbin hasn't done what they expected he would by now. Someone handed me the tissue box as a combination of tears and snot now covered my face. I tried so hard to hold it together, but the tears kept coming. Poor Jeff asked in every way he could think of about our chances of getting our Corbin back. He was begging for something positive to leave the meeting with, but it didn't come.

The last person to speak was the patient coordinator. She again told us that she would set up the tours and would be in to see us shortly. The decision was made with no further discussion. We'd been in this "Let Corbin show us" mode for weeks, and all of a sudden it's done. The decision had been made. I couldn't comprehend it. I was left with a blank look on my face and an empty feeling in my heart.

We left the meeting and started back toward Corbin's side of the floor. As soon as we made it through the entry doors to the ICU, I lost control and nearly fell to the floor. Everything that I had been holding in, all the strength I had been keeping up, was gone. Jeff stopped me and grabbed me in a bear hug before I hit the ground. I screamed and sobbed. I was so angry and felt defeated. How could this be happening after all he's made it through?

It felt like they were giving up and had decided it was too much effort to continue trying. Not long after, the coordinator came in and reassured us the long-term care facility was a great place and they would take good care of Corbin in the years to come. I hated her at that moment even though she was likely the sweetest woman. It was all too much to take in.

We pulled it together as best we could and went back to the room to see Corbin. Jeff was right when he said that we had to go back to day one. Corbin was here with us, and that's what mattered. I knew seeing him would help me. Being near him, hearing his machines, and feeling his warm hands always brought me comfort. Jeff and I had been reduced to nothing. The meeting had sucked the life right out of us.

There was comfort being in the room, but we were still struggling mightily. We needed a miracle and somehow, at that exact moment, we seemed to get one. Just like we had done for the previous three weeks, we talked to Corbin as if he was able to respond. Unfortunately, the conversation was one way. Until then. At that very moment, when we needed it more than any other moment prior, he responded to Jeff's voice. It was shocking.

We both turned to each other in disbelief. He didn't just open his eyes, he listened to him and responded by blinking. It was exactly what we needed. The heartbreak of the day still lingered, but this was what we needed to fill us with hope again. Hope that the doctors were wrong. Hope that we were experiencing a miracle. Hope that he was that kid that defied the odds. Once again, it didn't matter what they said. We saw Corbin respond, and it wasn't merely a reflex. He was there telling us, "Don't give up on me. I'm trying, and I'm still here."

14

THE TINIEST OF STRINGS

ime Stands Still - Journal Entry — July 25, 2018

Time felt like it stood still today with Corbin. No procedures no huge changes or progress. He still seems to be very much asleep. He's had about two minutes of support in about thirty-six hours of breathing on his own which is a big deal. He is also on full feeds with the tube. He will be off all morphine and sedation at 2 a.m. on Friday, so he's getting pretty low.

He's showing a few signs of withdrawals like yawning and the sweats. Besides that, he's actually handling it pretty well. I can't help but laugh every time he yawns. All I can picture is that kid who stayed up too late playing the video game and can't stop yawning. It looks like my Corbin again when he does it.

We're going to give it the weekend, and then we will visit the idea of a trach and G-tube in his stomach for feeding at the beginning of next week. So once again, it's the waiting game. Three weeks ago at this time

I was sitting in a waiting room along with about twenty of his family members and friends to see if he even survived his next set of surgeries that he was rushed into as soon as the helicopter landed. I sit alone with Corbin tonight, but I'm so thankful that I can still hold his warm hand in mine. I am thankful that I can still tell him I love him, and I'm still hopeful that someday he will be able to do the same back.

The 25th was another one for the ages. Jeff and Angie had come back down for the afternoon. I went to the back of the room and let them have their space with Corbin. It felt like my room, but I knew I needed to give them space when they were there. I had slept in that room as long as Corbin had, so essentially I had squatters' rights. I was living out of a small backpack and a public bathroom.

My mom and Jenn were headed down for the day. So, when they texted that they had arrived, I told Jeff I'd take them and go next door for lunch so they could have some time alone to visit. They were going to be leaving in the next hour, so it was easier to keep everyone separate.

I left and joined them for lunch, and soon after Paul texted that he was there to visit too so I told him to join us. We all had a nice visit, and everyone stayed for a few hours. I texted Jeff as we were leaving the cafeteria to let him know that we were headed back over. I made sure everyone stayed in the waiting room while I went in so we could switch shifts with no issues.

As I approached Corbin's room, a nurse who I had gotten pretty familiar with stopped me and said she felt like she needed to tell me what had happened while I was gone. She explained that Angie sat by Corbin's side holding his hand and sharing information that should have remained within the family. She proceeded to ask for the social worker to see if she was agreeable with getting me kicked out of Corbin's room during her visits so she could have private time with him.

I was seething. How dare she! I had been so patient, but that was it. The gloves were off. I couldn't understand how she could think of herself over everyone else. She wanted to ban a mother from her critical child's hospital room. It was just unfathomable.

I entered the room with what I'm sure was a look that could kill. A terse hi and bye were all that was exchanged before they scampered out of the room. Once they left, I went to the waiting room to bring everyone in. I explained what had happened and no one could believe what they heard. I walked everyone to Corbin's room and asked the nurse to call the social worker.

The social worker advised me that a parent can't be banned unless there's a court order. Parents can ban other people, however, and that's all I needed to hear. She'd crossed too many lines, and if she thought she was going to get between me and my child that was the last straw. I had Angie banned from the room. Jenn visited for a while and then started her long drive home. My mother had booked the hotel next door for three nights, so she was still visiting as well as Paul.

A few hours later, the social worker came back in and explained that she'd called Jeff and told him about the ban. He argued vehemently. When he knew he couldn't change it, he decided to play tit for tat and banned every other person from Corbin's room. Everyone? He's banning Corbin's siblings, his grandmother, Paul, and Tanna who helped save his life? My mother and Paul were then asked to leave. They were so hurt. My mother stayed the night at the hotel as planned but had to cancel the rest of her stay.

Once again, it was just Corbin and me in the room. I was really angry. He was lashing out at me, but in actuality he was hurting Corbin. Corbin needed the people he knew loved and cared about him. People he might recognize and who might trigger something for him. These were the people that mattered to Corbin, and Jeff's petty spite took it all away.

I tried to stay positive and be thankful for what I had, but I couldn't understand the selfishness. How can anything be more important than Corbin? My stress level was at the boiling point, and I wondered how I was going to tell Grace that she couldn't come back in and see her brother?

Two Kids One Hospital - Journal Entry — July 26, 2018

Corbin will be off all sedation in an hour. His morphine was shut off earlier today. He has been more alert as the day has gone on. Poor kid has been vomiting a lot tonight. His feeds were increased pretty fast and they think that's the cause, so food is on hold for now. He's having some symptoms of withdrawals, and that could be part of it as well. He is still breathing on his own with the vent for back up if he needs it.

Grace returned from field hockey camp today but got delayed seeing Corbin. She was hit pretty hard in the foot with a ball, so we ended up in the ER at Children's. I explained that she was allowed to spend the night and didn't need to get hurt and admitted to hang out here. She's fine though cut, bruised, sprained, and she's on crutches. The great news was when we finally got back up to see Corbin, he was the most alert he's been during the entire three weeks.

His eyes were open and when I got beside him, he turned his eyes in my direction and looked right at me. It is crazy how you can see so much in someone's eyes. I've seen the doctors lift his eyelids and check his pupils. There was no life in them for so long. They were empty. It was different tonight.

His face is still black and blue and beat up, but his eyes were the Corbin I know. There was so much life in them! I've missed seeing them more than I could ever express. I was so happy that Grace got to see that life in him also. It was very hard for her to leave him and go to camp, so to come back to that was so special.

It was a long night. He has a breathing tube in through his mouth and a large neck brace keeping his neck fractures stabilized. He has broken bones everywhere and is not easy to move. So, in addition to needing a group of nurses in the room to remove the brace, wash the pads, and change the sheets, there was also the fear of him choking. He was always kept in a slightly elevated bed position, and it's not like he could move to sit up or turn his head when the vomiting started.

It was the last day of field hockey camp and Jeff was supposed to pick Grace up. I had no choice but to tell her about the ban. I didn't know what I was going to do with her. I knew she planned on coming back to the hospital to see her brother, but she wasn't going to be allowed to.

She begged me to have Jenn come get her as she was furious with her father. Jenn agreed and made the hour drive to Dartmouth and then the almost three-hour drive back to Boston to bring Grace to me. Grace called her Dad to voice her disgust, and whatever she said to her father got him to at least lift the ban on siblings.

Grace was in rough shape though. She played a game that day and took a close contact direct hit to her foot. It was swollen and bloody. She had refused medical care at camp so she could get back to the hospital as fast as she could. I met her in the lobby, and we went straight to the ER. Living in a hospital does have its advantages here and there.

As soon as she got to the room, you could see the relief on her face. She needed to be back with Corbin and see that he was doing okay. She had such a huge surprise getting to see Corbin with his eyes open. That feeling never got old, and it gave us so much hope. There was no blank stare. He was making actual eye contact. They say eyes are the window to your soul, and I believed it then. He couldn't speak or move his body but looking in his eyes was all we needed to know that Corbin was there, and he was coming back strong.

We all went to bed with new hope and felt as if there would be more to come in the days ahead. In the middle of the night the withdrawals kicked in and poor Corbin threw up from 2 a.m. to 11 a.m. It was awful projectile vomiting that couldn't be blocked even with a breathing tube down his throat. He opened his eyes and looked at me as if to ask, "Why is this happening, Mom?"

He can't tell me, "Mom I'm in pain. Mom it's coming. I'm going to throw up." He just looks at me panic-stricken and can't say a word. The process of moving Corbin to change bedding and changing his neck brace took lots of time with multiple hands on deck. Within the first hour of seeing how bad it was getting, stacks of clean bedding were brought in as well as extra pads for his neck brace.

I sat beside him with a pile of towels waiting to try to contain the mess when it started. Keeping it out of the neck brace and spare the sheets if possible was my objective. Then, the nurses would take over, and I headed to the sink with the brace pads and scrubbed them, so he had clean ones for the next time. It started happening so often that the pads weren't drying in time, so I then began washing them and drying them with a blow dryer. I so wanted to take his pain away.

Just as quickly as that, he woke up on Friday morning awake and bright-eyed again. Jeff got there later in the day, and you could cut the tension it was so thick. Grace stayed in the back of the room with her foot up and was very short with Jeff. I wasn't happy, but I wanted anyone who might help pull Corbin in the room trying so I dealt with it. My mother was like a second mom to Corbin. He spent a lot of time with her growing up and still did. I knew that she should have been there with him that day if she wasn't banned, but FaceTime was the next best thing.

Cohen was with my mom FaceTiming. So, we held the phone up, and Cohen talked about all the things he wanted to show him and all the things he needed help with. He told Corbin that he needed to get better. Corbin stared right at the phone and even followed it with his eyes. He did the same with us. He looked for each of us when we talked. It sure felt like a miracle to me.

He is having other side effects from the vomiting like no more feeding, less urine output, and the risk of dehydration or infections like UTI. They are worried that other issues could be causing the vomiting so they're looking into that. He even squeezed my hand when I asked him to.

No sleep - Journal Entry — July 29, 2018

It's day twenty-five and, apparently, three and a half weeks of sleeping was enough for Corbin. He has been awake for the majority of the last twenty-four hours. Lots of ups and downs. It's heartbreaking to have him look at me and know he's trying to tell me something's wrong, but he can't say the words. His eyes and body movements are very clear that something is bothering him.

He's on new anti-nausea medicine that seems to help but nothing is helping to keep anything in his stomach. As soon as they turn the suction off to his stomach, he vomits. So, no feeds again for now. The scary part is wondering if this is only withdrawals or something more. They are running tests to see if it's his pancreas or blocked intestines, and making sure tubes are in the right place. You can tell the tubes in his mouth and down his throat are starting to really irritate him and for good reason.

This kid does not want to close his eyes. I can't go to the back of the room to sleep or let him out of my sight if he's awake. I didn't know if looking into his eyes was something I would ever see again, and I don't want to miss a second of it. I think Corbin is aware enough that he doesn't want to close his eyes and be alone.

Last night, his eyes would start to get heavy and close partially, so I would kiss him and tell him goodnight. Then, he would open them right back up and stare at me. So, I would stand there and talk to him, and it happened again. We did this routine four times.

Several of us, including the nurses, have seen the way he tries to move his mouth. We all believe that he's trying to say something. I think by the way he looks at me, squeezes my hand when I ask, and moves his mouth that he's trying to speak to us. I know it's going to take time and we're still living day by day, but I definitely have a newfound hope after seeing all the amazing things he's already doing.

The last few days had been so draining. Corbin was off nutrition, and he was losing weight. He was still going through withdrawals, and no one had slept. Grace and I were there alone. We couldn't get a break for anyone else to come in and help because no one was allowed. Jeff started only showing up for a few hours every other day, so it was up to us to man the watch around the clock.

The icing on the cake came when the nurse pulled me out of Corbin's room and asked me to come out to the waiting area, where a police officer served me court paperwork. Jeff and Angie are taking me to court to get her reinstated back in the room. I'm not sure how much can be put on a person's plate before they break but we were getting mighty close to finding out.

Three Days Written Into One - Journal Entry — July 31, 2018

On Sunday, I woke up to a bunch of nurses moving Corbin until he started throwing up. It was day four of miserable withdrawals, and it feels like he's regressing. He's not as alert, and he's not staying awake long. He has strange body twitching and is dripping in sweat. He's suffering, and it's making me crazy. When he was sedated it was bad, but he didn't know. Now that he's more aware, I can see the pain in his eyes. It's an awful feeling to not be able to make his pain go away.

They feel that his bowels are backed up, so they are working on that. The skin on his neck and chin started breaking down from all the vomiting into the neck brace. It's a different kind of bad.

Monday, Corbin is more alert again. They want to give him a trach and G-tube this week so that means, we're getting off of all the drugs before he goes back on them for another week and we start the process all over again. He's on a small amount of pressure support and is basically breathing on his own. He has so much damage to the airway though, they are afraid if they try to pull the tube out, they won't be able to get the tube back down if needed. So, trying is too dangerous.

Tuesday it finally felt like he's getting out of the withdrawals. His bowels are so backed though that they can see it on X-ray, and they believe that's what's not allowing him to tolerate anything in his stomach. He did start IV nutrition again today since he had nothing since Friday morning.

His trach and G-tube surgeries are scheduled for Thursday and that's another stress. He will have to be put back on the same meds, he's withdrawing from for another week. Once they get a trach, they have to be paralyzed and sedated for five days for it to heal correctly. This is a long road. He has survived the unthinkable, and he's still fighting hard. So, this is just one more hurdle to add to the list.

Corbin looked like he was wasting away. When they would take his johnny off to change him, he looked like a Prisoner of War from the end of World War II. He was nothing but skin and bones. His full rib cage and his hip bones were sticking out. His stomach was sunken, and his legs had shrunk to half the size.

Corbin was getting no nutrition, and his bodily functions weren't working. He stopped looking at me as well. He was developing sores on his body, and it felt like we were going backward. It was so painful to see him like this.

I was becoming a mother not to be messed with. On top of watching my son waste away, I now had to find a lawyer and set up meetings outside of the room to conference on the phone with them because there was no way I was leaving the hospital.

The patient coordinator was pushing me to visit Franciscans Rehab, but I'd done some research and it seemed to be a long-term care facility. There was no way that's where Corbin was going. He was not going to sit in a bed for the rest of his life, over my dead body. If he didn't qualify for Spaulding, then I would find somewhere else.

I spent the few minutes a day I could spare searching the different rehab options all over the country. What kind of care and technology they had to support pediatric brain injuries, what facilities they had for parents, and how long the flights to and from

New Hampshire would be knowing I still had three other children I would need to care for. I remember the coordinator saying, "But that's so far!" Far? Does that matter when it's your child's life? I would have traveled any length to help Corbin.

They tried to convince me that he was going to be too much to care for at home, and he would have to live in a facility. I made it very clear, that was never going to happen. I was going home with that child, bedridden, in a wheelchair, or walking. He was never going to be left for someone else to take care of him.

The reality of it all was that my plate was overflowing and if I didn't find something resembling balance, I was going to end up hospitalized upstairs from Corbin. There were times that I feared the medical staff was sizing me up for a straitjacket. I considered advising them that size medium in a sky-blue color would work just fine. The stress of missing my other children and worrying that I wasn't doing enough for them was killing me. I was also concerned about their mental wellbeing trying to deal with all of this and living in different homes. I was holding it all together by the tiniest of strings.

15

THE UGLY SIDE OF IT ALL

*O*ne month - *Journal Entry — August 1, 2018*

     One month ago, our lives were all changed forever. I'm going to look back on these entries someday and realize that one month seemed like a long time, when it was just a blink of an eye in the whole scheme of this. It becomes clearer every day what a long road this is going to be.

     Not much has changed with Corb today. He had a CT scan to see if they could figure out if something else was going on that was preventing him from being able to keep anything in his stomach. I still haven't received the results. I'm waiting up for the night rounds to get answers and what the next course of action will be.

     Corbin is scheduled for surgery at 7:30 a.m. tomorrow. He will be getting the trach and G-tube put in. He will have to be paralyzed and sedated for three to five days until it heals. I've been told the weaning off of the drugs will be done a little differently this time, so he won't suffer so much.

I am in awe of this child. The pain and suffering he is fighting through every single day is just incredible. And it really is a fight. You can see it in his eyes and the expressions he tries to make. The scars he already has are almost too many to count. As if he wasn't special enough before this, now he's like a living miracle. I'm so proud of the fight in him.

Corbin was doing better. He was more alert again. They assured me that as much as I fought it, this surgery was for the best. I just wanted him to stop being tortured. The trach was something I really didn't want. He was basically breathing on his own, so I didn't understand why they needed to cut a big hole in his throat. The breathing specialist said daily how well he was doing on pressure support alone. He was barely using the breathing machine at all.

The issue was if they pulled the breathing tube out and for some reason he couldn't handle breathing on his own, with his esophagus so badly damaged they wouldn't be able to get an emergency line down. Then, they would have to do an unplanned tracheotomy which is not ideal. They assured me that he probably wouldn't need the trach long-term which seemed especially irritating. If he doesn't need it for long, then why don't we give him a little longer to heal before he is drugged and has a big hole put in his throat? After days of pushing me and convincing me that it would be okay, I gave in.

I knew he needed the G-tube in his stomach, and I was okay with that. Nutrition through the one in his nose wasn't working, so this was the next best option. I imagined the improvements we'd see when his body had what it needed to heal itself. I always feared watching him get wheeled away into surgery. I was always scared it could be the last time that I would see him. He was never out of the woods. He had new challenges every single day and being put under always brought more.

After surgery they told me that they would not be sedating him or paralyzing him as they had originally explained. They said he doesn't move enough to need it, and if we can keep him safe without the drugs that's what's best. They did leave the feeding tube that went through his nose but moved it further down to his intestines.

His CT scan showed no blockage from his bowels or any other source of why he can't tolerate the feeds. So, they've decided to bypass the stomach and feed right into the intestines. The tube is clogged though, so tomorrow he will have to have a new tube placed so he can start feeds. They believe this will give his stomach time to heal while still getting him the nutrition he needs.

He was opening his eyes about fifteen minutes after he got back from surgery and has been alert and awake the majority of the day. He was making all sorts of movements with his mouth and even sticking his tongue out at Gracie.

As a way to make the day just a bit more stressful, today was court on top of Corbin's surgery. My lawyer made sure that I could telephone in instead of having to leave to go back to NH. I didn't know when Corbin would be out of surgery however, and I hoped it didn't fall when I had to be away on the phone. I was angry that Jeff was choosing to be in court instead of being at the hospital with Corbin, but I've come to expect very little from him and, therefore, I'm never disappointed. Nonetheless, I was angry that my attention and time were being pulled away from Corbin on such an important day for this.

On the bright side, Jeff had lifted the ban on other family members being able to see Corbin. Though, that may have been at the suggestion of his lawyer, it still was a positive event. When tragedies and trying times like this happen, it brings out the best or the worst in people.

For most of the people involved it brought us together. Any past issues were put aside, and Corbin was the priority. Jeff's sister Christine and I had our ups and downs and hadn't spoken much in years, but she loved Corbin like her own. What had happened between us in the past didn't matter. She had called me before the surgery and knew that I might need to be out of the room when he was coming back. So, she offered to come down and be there for him in case I couldn't. I jumped at the offer.

Corbin finished quickly. I got word that he was on his way back to the room at the same time my lawyer said I needed to call in. So I told her I couldn't. She completely agreed and said she would handle it. My mom was there with her, and she said she would explain to the judge the seriousness of the matter and that my presence was needed with Corbin much more than at court.

Court didn't matter to me the second Corbin was back in the room. He looked so good! His face had been so covered in tubes before the surgery. I had gotten used to seeing him like that and forgot how handsome he was now that the only thing on his face was a small tube through his nose and all of that facial hair that aged him tremendously. I wish he could have seen himself! He would have told me that he could probably go into a store and buy beer since he looked so much older.

Corbin and Grace loved to tease each other, and it didn't stop here. She hung over him, talking to him, and he reacted to it all even right out of surgery. To see him stick out his tongue at her was hysterical, and she melted. You couldn't show us any MRI that would convince us that our Corbin wasn't in there; slowly but surely emerging.

He's Just Incredible - Journal Entry — August 3, 2018

I've been so hesitant to post any pictures of Corbin. His first few weeks were pretty gruesome. I'm sure that half the people on here would not care to see how bad it really was. It wasn't for the weak stomach that's for sure. I don't have a weak stomach and still when I look back now, it's hard to take in. I decided to post a recent picture of Corbin because he looks so good.

You'll never appreciate how good he looks unless you saw him post-accident but, in any case, it shows his eyes. It shows his determination. Sometimes, I feel like it's just me who sees him trying to communicate when he looks at me but it's not. All of his nurses say the same thing. There is no blank stare. He has things to say. His brain is trying so hard. I have no doubt. He moves his mouth when I talk to him. He wants to talk back.

Corbin started his feeds again today and, so far so good. They have bypassed his stomach and it's going straight into the intestines, so hopefully, that will help him tolerate them for now. He has been fighting a fever all day. He spikes to close to 104. He gets covered in ice packs, which seems like absolute torture to me. I call his room the igloo. It might as well be the middle of winter. I dress in pants and sweatshirts all day long. While he is cooking like he's on a beach in Mexico.

He's on antibiotics, but they might need to add a broad-spectrum med if they can't figure out what's causing it. On a good note. Once the trach is five days old, they are going to try to test him off the vent. He has been on the lowest support, and they don't believe he needs it. So, that's a huge step in the right direction.

This kid is incredible, and I have no doubt that he's going to continue to make us all so proud.

Corbin was blowing us away, more and more, every single day. He continued to have his daily struggles, but he was trying valiantly to come back. His fever was nerve-wracking to us all, and they couldn't figure out where the infection was coming from. They feared it was from his brain and that would have been a devastating setback.

We knew the bolt that was monitoring the brain was a risk. He was already on a daily antibiotic through IV, and now they wanted to add a stronger med to culture some of the fluid that had been draining from his head. Meningitis was a big fear, and that risk brought in a whole new team of doctors daily to discuss the concerns and treatment options.

As the day progressed Corb fought with a high fever all night and day. The treatment was to put him on a broad-spectrum of antibiotics, and he is alternating with Tylenol, Motrin, and morphine. After more than 24 hours of hovering right under 104 degrees, his temperature finally dropped to normal.

I don't think you can really say that there is a good time for a catastrophic accident like this. Though, if you could control the timing, Corbin nailed it. The kids were on school vacation so with Cohen staying between my mom and Jeff's house, at least he wasn't being run back and forth to school and the countless activities he engages in. It also gave Grace the opportunity to be at the hospital full time with Corbin. She needed to be there just as Corbin needed her. To watch him stare at her was special. Everyone could see their bond. She would talk like there was no communication issue at all, and she would giggle in between while his eyes would follow her around the room.

It was so hard to see him struggle. I equate it to having a sick baby. They just look up at you with the red bloodshot eyes. You know they feel awful, but they can't tell you what hurts. As a mom, all you want to do is take away their pain and make them better. So, we let him rest when his eyes are closed, talk to him as much as we can when he wakes up, and keep a cool cloth on his forehead to make him as comfortable as we can.

The nagging nuisance of the court and lawyers are now becoming a daily presence. Angie had been pressing everyone about getting a lawyer. She made it very clear that she didn't want hospitals coming after her "assets" for Corbin's medical bills. I'd already asked the social worker, and she advised me that Children's doesn't do that.

Then, there was the issue of Corbin's medical insurance. I spoke with Jeff about it a few times, and we agreed to speak to a lawyer as long as we selected one and met with the lawyer together. I also reminded him that it would only be the two of us doing this.

Before I even hung up the phone, I received a text from Angie telling me that she's picked a lawyer and she has an appointment with him. She advised me that it would be an appointment that Jeff and I would not be at. I made it very clear that her terms were unacceptable. I would be calling lawyers but not before I told her clearly, that as Corbin's legal guardian no one, except me, had the right to hire a lawyer regarding my son. She said, "All three of us are Corbin's legal guardians," which is absolutely not true.

The most frustrating part was the energy that this took away from me. Each time I had to leave Corbin's room to call lawyers or fax documents, I expended what little energy I had left. My tank was running dry as it was and much like my infamous gas tank, I was running on fumes.

Everyone had lives and jobs, or they were home taking care

of my life, while Angie was spending countless hours thinking of only her own personal gain. Jeff stopped coming daily. Instead, he'd visit his son twice per week at most. Luckily, Paul had a flexible schedule and would come to visit almost every day. We always looked forward to his company.

16

A MIRACLE APPEARS
BEFORE OUR VERY EYES

More Progress - *Journal Entry* — *August 6, 2018*

Corb's fever has been under control. The samples run were cultured, and everything came back negative for a growing infection. So, there is no clue what caused it. It remains normal and under control, so that's where we stand.

Today was an awesome day. He's been tolerating his feeds great, and what a difference it's made in his level of alertness. You can see how much better he feels. He will be on full feeds by tomorrow morning. Slow and steady works well for Corbin. The eye doctors were able to dilate his eyes for the first time and saw no damage. They believe his vision will be fine.

A speech therapist came to work with him today. The task was quite simple, as she simply asked him to look at her instead of me, which he did. Then, she had yes and no cards which she held up and asked him *questions. It was incredible to see him communicating even in this rather primitive way. Even if he didn't regain speech, it became exciting that he could recognize and understand so we would be able to learn to communicate with him. He was very clearly answering yes and no and following commands.*

The therapist would have him open his mouth and stick his tongue out; this was something he had become very adept at previously. He was looking around the room at different voices he would hear instead of staying fixated on just one person. He was also making some expressions. I showed him a funny picture of himself, and he definitely smirked. It was such an awesome day to see so much from him!

Tomorrow he gets his first trach change, and then they will start testing him with no vent. They don't believe it should take long seeing that he's been breathing with the lowest setting almost this whole time. Once he has no vent, we can start moving him to a big recliner and many more positions. And once the trach is capped, we will be able to hear if he's able to talk. This kind of progress is what we live for.

To see his brain working was something we didn't know if we would ever get to witness. It made me realize that we move so fast in our daily lives and take so much for granted. Our bodies can breathe without thinking about it, our eyesight, chewing our food, jumping out of bed in the morning, even having the ability to talk. We do it all without a second thought, but Corbin couldn't do any of it. We didn't know from day to day what he would get back and what he would never regain.

Every day that we got to see improvement was a miracle. We knew, by this time, that the damage to his eye had healed, and he could see. His brain was firing and that was incredible. It meant that his brain was processing sound, interpreting, and correctly responding automatically and without hesitation. It seems so minor to most of us but this was for someone with a traumatic brain injury.

The speech therapist left us tools so when she wasn't there, we could work with Corbin. We had a sign with a big red NO and a big green YES. We could now ask Corbin, "Are you in pain? Are you tired? Are you scared? Do you love your mom?" He would finally communicate with us even on the simplest level, though he did seem to think about it when contemplating whether or not he loved his mom. Then, he smirked and he'd motion toward the yes sign. Even under these conditions, the kid made us laugh.

The speech therapist explained that Corbin couldn't currently talk even if he was ready since the trach was open. The trach had to be open to keep him hooked to the breathing machine. Once it was time to test breathing on his own, they would unhook the machine and put a cap over the trach. Only when its capped would we be able to hear the sound of his voice. I knew that he wanted to talk so badly by the way his mouth would move when I talked to him.

Too Excited - Journal Entry — August 7, 2018

My day started with Dr. Mooney waking me as he had been at 7 a.m. He's finally back from vacation, and I couldn't be happier. He asked how Corbin had been doing, and I explained everything that happened yesterday. He said, "I don't think you understand how huge that is." He explained that Corbin had to focus on us, hear us, process the information, which takes several parts of the brain, and then perform the action.

He was very honest and said with how severe his injuries were, there were plenty of doctors that didn't think he would even end up opening his eyes. He then repeated, "I don't know if you understand how huge this really is." Then we talked about some other out of state options for rehab including Chicago and Baltimore.

From there, Corbin had his first trach change which went well, and then they took him off the vent. He has spent all day to this point off of the breathing machine. They will put it on for bed tonight and as long as everything goes well, he'll go off it again tomorrow morning and then be off for good. That's the plan.

Next, neurology came in, and he was awake this time! He followed commands for many things including following different directions with his eyes, he opened his mouth, he squeezed her hand and then released, he lifted his left arm, he moved both legs and toes, and closed his eyes. It was incredible! He's very weak still so some of the movements were slight but, more importantly, he did and understood them all.

After that, his primary doctor, Brad, came in and said he spoke with the neuro team that had just been in the room. They were super impressed. He said, "You know sometimes doctors have these hush-hush conversations, but this wasn't like that. They were amazed by what Corbin was doing." Brad said all of the fellows have been watching Corbin since he got here. Some I've never even met, some observed via reports and images, but they have all been following him from day one.

Corbin's case is the talk of them all. "This isn't the kid that came in here a month ago. No one expected this, and everyone is beside themselves with what he's doing." I wanted to cry. If that's not enough to give you the hope to keep fighting and pushing through this, I don't know what is.

Brad then got on the phone with the physical therapist, who had met with Corbin a few times but wasn't at the hospital today. He will be back tomorrow, and he was so excited to hear the news. Brad said the PT will fill me in on how great this is when he comes to meet with me tomorrow, but he believes all this progress makes Corbin much closer to being a candidate for Spaulding. Then, they set me up to tour Spaulding.

Corbin has improved by leaps and bounds these past few days. If I had a graph of his progress, the past two days would be off the charts. Three weeks of relatively small increments of progress and the past two days pointing skyward. He's *that* kid. We still have such a long road and no idea what Corbin's full potential will be, but we're getting there day by day.

Besides our amazing nurses that were with us day in and day out, Dr. Mooney was my go-to guy. I always looked forward to our early morning meetings when he would wake me up, and I hated when he wasn't there. I didn't want any other doctor to make the decisions or to do anything else to Corbin without his approval. There was something I trusted about him. It always felt like he was taking care of Corbin like he would if it was his child. It was never standard protocol.

I knew it was huge. I wanted to hug him. Any improvement from the previous day was huge for me, but to hear him say it filled me with so much hope. It wasn't just a hopeful mother clinging to little things because she wanted to believe.

Then, we discussed therapy, and I expressed my desire for not sending him to a long-term care facility out of state. He agreed, though my mind was already made up regardless of his feelings. That poor patient coordinator put up a good fight. I made a deal with her, I told her that I would see her facility if she made an appointment at Spaulding for me as well. I would go see the ones out of state, but I wanted Corbin at Spaulding. I didn't care what I had to do to get him there.

The day continued to get better when Brad came to talk to

me. He said there will be papers written on Corbin's case. This is like something they had never seen before. The damage to Corbin's brain was so severe he shouldn't be doing any of this. He had shearing in his brain which isn't just bruising or swelling. It's when parts of the brain actually tear, and there is no explanation as to why he is experiencing the progress we are seeing. No explanation perhaps except love, hope, the support of thousands, and the refusal to accept no for an answer.

The Long Road - Journal Entry — August 9, 2018

So, the last few days have been filled with PT, OT, and speech therapy. They've had him up in a seated position on the edge of the bed twice now. It takes lots of support but he's trying hard. The sessions are exhausting for him, which can also be pretty difficult for me to watch. They are teaching me and Grace the moves as well so we can keep working on them throughout the day.

It's very hard to watch your once strong young teenager not be able to hold his own head up. One of the things they ask him to do is give a thumbs up. They asked ten times yesterday, and he did it once. Today he did it four times. Those are the small gains they want to see. Now when I say he gave a thumbs up, it means he moves his thumb from the clenched position up about half an inch. It doesn't have to be perfect but him comprehending it and trying is huge.

It's times like that you realize how long this road is really going to be. It's like we just typed the directions into the navigation and still have a cross country trip to set out on.

Corbin is doing so well breathing on his own that the machine has been moved right out of his room. There are a few other medical issues they're trying to figure out, but they have a team working hard to get him accepted to Spaulding. We're waiting to hear more about that. He's getting pretty close to the move day if things continue progressing. He is on a course of antibiotics until the sixteenth. So, he might have to stay until those are done, but it could be sooner if everything lines up correctly.

August 8th was a personal victory day, and a day of begging by a desperate mother. I had my appointment at Spaulding. As much as I wanted to go, I hated to leave Corbin. Physical therapy was scheduled for that day, and they were going to try to sit Corbin up. I didn't want to miss any of these milestones, but I knew how important this appointment was, so Grace stayed with Corb and promised to take lots of pictures to keep me up to date.

I took a cab, so I didn't have to deal with the anxiety I felt the last time I drove. It was so strange being away from the hospital for only the third time in over a month. It felt like my first day in the real world, and it felt more like I was in a foreign country instead of Boston. The traffic, the lights, the people going in every direction, and me gazing out the window of the car. I don't believe that I could have maneuvered through the streets on my own.

I looked at all the people hustling up the busy sidewalk, attempting to cross the street, and I wondered if they were barely surviving like I was. Did they have their own personal battles they were fighting? We get dressed each morning, do our hair, our face, and our teeth. We enter the day and others may be unaware of the personal battles we are fighting. We simply see the world through our own lenses, likely unaware of what the person next to us may be battling. Did I look like one of those people going about my day, or was my pain visible on my face?

Spaulding was absolutely beautiful! It was such a gorgeous building right on the water. The pediatric floor was small. It only had twelve rooms, and that was a big part of the reason that it would be hard to get Corbin accepted. Like Children's, people come from all over the country, and the world, to have their children treated there. To be accepted, the child needs to be able to participate in three different therapies a day, four to five days a week.

I was willing to beg to get him into the crown jewel of all rehab facilities. I was given a tour of the floor by a nurse who was more than happy to answer all of my questions. I told her about Corbin, how bad he was, and how far he'd come. I explained how fast he was improving and how badly I wanted him there to continue to improve. She sounded pretty confident Corbin could qualify, but the decision couldn't be made until he was ready to be transferred and they knew exactly where he was in therapy at that time.

I'll take that answer as maybe. Not yes but it certainly wasn't a no. I felt great when I left. I knew it was the place for Corbin, and I was going to make sure it happened.

On my way back to the hospital, I checked my email and saw an urgent message from my attorney. I hesitated to open the email as I didn't want anyone or anything to rain on my parade. If there is such a thing as opening an email slowly, that's what I did. I carefully read the email and learned that the court had decided in my favor. Angie would have no contact at Children's or at any rehab facility he stays at in the future. This was one less issue that I had to deal with, one less lawyer, and it was one less thing to keep me away from Corbin.

He was doing so well with his breathing, but the therapy was taking its toll. As excited as we would get for the highs, the fear is never too far away. As often as we would see him answer by looking at yes and no, he would just as frequently take ten attempts to get things correct at other times. What if he's regressing? What if this is all he'll ever do? As good as things feel one minute, they could go in reverse just as quickly.

17

THE DAY WE THOUGHT MAY NEVER COME

*W*e're Moving - *Journal Entry — August 10, 2018*

I have been told that Corbin is now the healthiest kid in the ICU, and we will probably be moving to another floor of the hospital at some point today. But . . . it's just a pit stop because CORBIN'S GOING TO SPAULDING!! Spaulding has accepted him, and as soon as they have a room he will be moving. This could be as soon as Monday!!

In a span of only five weeks, we've been told to say goodbye to him, doctors being surprised that he made it through the night those first few nights, being told we're up to a "fifty-fifty chance of making it through the night," being told they don't know if he'll ever wake up, and all the other horrible stages imaginable. Look at him now. He is being transferred to one of the best rehabilitation centers in the country. Some serious tears of joy this morning!

I was so excited that I had to share the news instantly! It was a dream come true! In only thirty-eight of the longest days imaginable, Corbin went from being the highest risk, worst injured person on the floor to the healthiest. What a miracle. I couldn't contain the relief I felt, the first easy breath I had taken in five weeks. He's going to get the best rehab the country has to offer and, best of all, he will be coming home with us when it's all over. If we had survived this far, we had the rest.

It was one of the most positively emotional days since this whole nightmare began. There was no way I was going to let Corbin just go sit in a facility that wasn't going to push him. I know that he is now going to reach his full potential, and then he's coming home. I had been researching, pushing, and fighting every day to get Corbin somewhere that was going to give him his best possible chance of recovery and the fullest life possible. To learn that Spaulding, my first choice was happening, brought tears to my eyes.

They told us that we would move upstairs once they had everything ready for us. Grace and I had our work cut out for us! We had Corb's room full of posters, decorations, clothes, bedding, and then a sleep room where we kept our back up clothes and toiletries. We couldn't keep that room, so we needed to pack up our temporary lives and move.

Then, reality sank in as we realized that we were leaving Rosa and the people who saved Corbin. My happy tears soon turned to tears of goodbye and uncertainty. I tried to stay positive, as I knew this was the next step. The next step was finally happening, when I didn't know for weeks before, if we'd ever get to take it.

We packed and emptied that ICU room into a little cart, and we waited. Late afternoon, they came in and said, "Time to go." I'm not sure I've ever had such mixed emotions. Rosa seemed happy for us but a little sad as well. I sensed that she was going to miss us as much as we would miss her. She packed up his machines, and we started the trek upstairs with Rosa at the head of Corbin's bed like a proud mom.

When we got to his room, we said our goodbyes pretty fast. Rosa promised to keep in touch and visit us often. I had been crying about five hours straight at that point; it was a mix of the happiest and saddest emotions all in one. I never wanted to lose contact with Rosa. She had become part of our family. We had spent most of the last five weeks together, and I watched her take care of Corbin in ways I wanted to, in ways a mother would take care of her child.

She protected him and loved him, and I felt like I owed her so much. I was so thankful she was the one working that first day and so thankful she had that instant connection with my son. As I wrote my post that night, tears poured down my face. Grace looked at me and said, "You're writing about Rosa, aren't you?" She was the hardest part of leaving the ICU.

The new room made us feel spoiled. It felt like we were in a luxury hotel room. It didn't feel as comfortable as the ICU that first night, but we knew we'd adjust. We didn't know how long we'd be there knowing that Corbin still needed to get the trach out, tolerate meds better, and get off his antibiotics before we could move to Spaulding.

Spaulding also didn't have a bed at that time, and we couldn't get any sort of answer when they would have one. It could be days, weeks, or even months. We didn't know how long we'd be in our new home, but we were excited to have our own shower and bathroom. No more brushing our teeth in the waiting room bathroom and now being able to eat in the room was a big plus. I explained the move to Corbin without much reaction from him. I didn't want him to be scared or confused, but he handled the move fine.

Thank You - Journal Entry — August 11, 2018

I have to start this post with the biggest THANK YOU that I could possibly give! THANK YOU to our family and friends for taking the time to put on that massive fundraiser last night. I know how much work and time they put into it, while they all still have their own busy lives going on. THANK YOU to everyone for their generous donations! The amount of time and thoughtfulness to put baskets together, to make signs, and the money everyone donated.

THANK YOU to everyone who came to support Corbin!! I was told there were 500 people there. I'm speechless. I could never put into words how much gratitude I have for all of you. I feel so blessed to have the love and support from every one of you

We were going to try to FaceTime so Corbin could see everyone there last night, but he fell asleep early and woke up with a fever and vomiting. Luckily, I was sent lots of pictures and videos so when he gets up today, I'll show him all of them.

We are blessed by the most amazing family. Not everyone could be there supporting us in person every day, but they busted their butts supporting us in so many ways. They also thought so much further ahead than I did. They knew the countless updates that our home would need to accommodate Corbin when he came home, the specialized care he could need, and the fact that I had no job to support four children at this point.

So, our Aunt Jan, who is Paul's amazing mother and Jenn came up with the idea of a fundraiser event. The support and interest grew so much that it had to be moved from a local restaurant to a hotel conference center. People donated the most amazing items including skis, massages, lottery tickets, Red Sox tickets, handmade quilts, and more. It took a huge team of family and friends to pull it all together. It was a well-executed operation with credit card payment options, people working the door, an auction, team Corbin shirts and gear for sale, and a beautiful floral centerpiece, all with funny pictures of Corbin in them. It was amazing.

I'd been asked if I wanted to go and I really did. I wanted to thank everyone personally and wanted everyone to know how much it all meant to us, but I couldn't bring myself to leave Corbin. Paul said it would probably be too overwhelming for me. He said, "You have no idea how many people are going to be there."

As we've come to expect, the night wasn't without drama. Jeff wasn't happy that his family was together working with mine on all of these events. Jeff and Angie thought everyone in his family should have turned their backs on me, but he failed to see that I was the only parent supporting Corbin. I was the one who slept by his side every single night from day one, the one who quit my job, the one who wasn't seeing all my kids every day.

Everyone knew Corbin was my priority, and no one was keeping me from taking care of my child. It was really a sad situation. Jeff and a few family members showed up late, all wearing shirts that Angie designed because they refused to wear the ones we selected to sell. They stayed a short time until Angie caused a scene complaining that Grace was ignoring her little sister. Her whole brood stormed out after her. Except for the unnecessary drama, life felt right that night and, overall, the picture was filled with promise.

Week 6 - Journal Entry — August 16, 2018

Things on the tenth floor move much slower than in the ICU. Sort of feels like Ground Hog day up here, as one day seems like the next and similar to the one before. We still have no word on an open bed at Spaulding, but they have been trying some new things with his rehab here. Today they used a lift and sat Corbin in a recliner with his feet up. He lounged and watched preseason football for about two hours. He did great and really seemed to enjoy it.

We left his door open, and he turned to look every time someone walked by. Grace pulled a chair right up beside him and worked on her new bracelet making hobby. They hung out together like old times. It was sweet to watch. She really doesn't ever want to leave his side.

Corbin got another MRI today. They tried to do it yesterday, but he wouldn't stop moving his leg and trying to turn his head. So, they didn't get any images. Today they sedated him, so it was much smoother. A doctor on the floor said the images were the same as the last ones, as they expected. Neurology will be able to share more detail. The spine doctor is coming to discuss how much longer he'll have the collar on, and then the infectious disease doctors will advise if they feel comfortable taking him off of the antibiotics for meningitis.

As soon as he stops these antibiotics, we will start a different one that he will have to take every day for two years. He also got two vaccines in the last few days that he wouldn't normally have at this age, but he has to have them since they removed his spleen.

I got to change his trach, which was interesting. It is so strange to see a hole in his throat and then shove a plastic device down it. They said I did great, and it felt pretty comfortable. I'm trying to learn as much as I can, and as much as they'll let me do in here. That way, I can take care of him when we go home.

It was a typical day on the 15th. Grace and I went down to the cafeteria for lunch once Corbin fell asleep. We had watched every movie possible, and the highlight of the day was normally when therapy would come in and work with him. It was exciting to see what they pushed him to do next.

The night was pretty typical as well. Paul was there to visit so he, Grace, and I sat around talking and kept Corbin entertained. Though Jeff hadn't visited in several days, he was in Boston, so he stopped up to visit.

It made Corbin happy to see Jeff, so I was glad when he showed up. Jeff, Cohen, and Keira came into the room, and Corbin lit up to see his dad and the kids. It was kind of sad to see the way Keira looked at me though. Before any of this, she would run in and hug me, and now she barely dared to look at me. She was even hesitant to come and see Grace because she was sitting next to me on the other side of the room. It was pretty clear that her mind had been poisoned.

Cohen, of course, came over and hugged me, and then he proceeded to tell me about his day. Besides Keira's discomfort it began as a good visit. Everyone was in a good mood, talking and joking, and telling Jeff all the new things going on. About ten minutes after they got there, Keira hugged Grace, and they started to goof around and be silly. She loosened up and started to fool with me also. Almost instantly, Angie appeared in the doorway and yelled, "That's not okay, Jeff!"

It startled me so much I jumped.

Jeff yelled back at her, "RELAX!"

She barked back, "GET THE KIDS OUT OF THERE!"

Those kids, one of them being mine, looked as shocked as I

did. Keira ran right out. Poor Cohen dropped his head, and he left the room without even hugging me goodbye. Jeff gave me this nasty look and said sarcastically, "You're the best. Thanks, Sadie."

There was no love lost between any of us, and it was getting uglier by the day. We were all stunned. Grace said that she knew Angie was right outside the room. She had noticed that her dad left the door wide open when he came in, and then she noticed Angie watching the whole visit through the blinds. Apparently, she didn't respect the no-contact order, and I was furious. What kind of person causes a scene like that in a hospital room?

How dare she treat either of my sons with such disrespect. I called the social worker and my lawyer right away. I was assured that if anyone spotted her on his floor again, they would have security escort her away.

I was becoming an expert at suctioning Corbin. I would stop the machines from beeping and get him suctioned before a nurse could even make it in the room. They assured me that it wouldn't hurt him, but I wasn't sure how that was true.

If it did hurt, Corbin never let on. It was easier than I expected. They said I did it perfectly, so one more thing checked off the list. I got trained in the different sizes, the different tubes, and in cleaning them. A few more practices and I'd be a pro.

18

IMPROVING IN LEAPS AND BOUNDS

Friday Journal Entry — August 17, 2018

When Corbin woke up this morning his eyes were brighter and more curious. He was tracking everyone around the room, more so than he had been. They moved him to the recliner again, and he looked so proud of himself. Then, PT came in and it was incredible to watch. His left side is much looser and more flexible. He was doing so much on command, over and over. He's also moving his left side so much more than he had been. He kicks his left leg around all day long. We think he's trying to escape from the room.

He was so pleased with himself today. The rest of the day we would ask him to open and close his hand, and he did it over and over. He was also moving his mouth a lot today. So, we capped his trach thinking he might want to try to say something, but he was not quite ready yet, I guess.

He made a lot more facial expressions today also. He was definitely trying to smile. Both sides of his mouth were slightly curling up. I got quite a few raised eyebrows. It's such a Corbin thing and makes us laugh.

We both needed this day. We were feeling each other's frustrations but today was like a new light switch turned on. We're both feeling energized and ready to keep pushing.

Corbin's right arm had been curled up to his chest for some time with a closed fist. He reminded me of Napoleon or even former presidential candidate Robert Dole, whose arm was injured in a war accident during World War II. It was starting to get hard to move it when he tried to straighten it or move his fingers. The doctors explained that his muscles could shorten if it stayed that way for too long. We would try to unroll his fingers and put rolled-up face cloths in his hands so he couldn't make such a tight fist. It was always something.

I was worried that he wasn't progressing fast enough, and Spaulding would change their mind. I was constantly worrying that a new MRI would show something bad or concerned he'd get some new infections and we'd never get to leave. It always sat in the back of my head to get me nerved up, even when things seemed to be flowing smoothly.

I had been looking forward to having them cap his trach since he got it. I really needed to hear his voice. Corbin had severe damage to his esophagus, and they didn't know if that would affect his ability to talk. So, I was dying to hear that beautiful voice and know that he still had it. I knew it may not happen like that, but I could hope and pray. It certainly wouldn't be the first miracle he'd pulled off.

I capped the trach and waited to see what happened. He

moved his mouth a little, but no sound emanated at all. It was fine. Corbin moved at his own pace, and if he was going to speak it would be on his terms.

Thumbs up - Journal Entry — August 18, 2018

Corbin had another great day. It seems like this switch has been turned on the last two days. Today he was lifting his arm right off the bed and reaching for us. At one point, he grabbed Gracie's hand and pulled it up toward his mouth, and then he opened his mouth like he wanted to bite her. We were laughing so hard. They have such a teasing relationship that this would be perfectly normal behavior with them. Then, we could see him trying really hard to smile, slightly lifting the corners of his mouth.

When we were getting ready to leave and I told him we would be right back, he grabbed my hand super tight. Next, he lifted his lip on one side and gave me the snarling Elvis lip. Then, he was reaching for my arm and pulling me close. It was pretty clear that he didn't want us to leave.

We left and got him some of his favorite movies to watch. When we returned the nurses moved him into the recliner. This is his third time in the chair. The first time he needed it reclined with pillows propped every-where to support him, but today he didn't even need any pillows around his head to support his neck. He's moving really fast with PT. I can only imagine the leaps and bounds he's going to make at Spaulding when it's for longer periods and more often.

He has quite the hairstyle going on because, as most of you know, it was pretty long before the accident and now it's super long. Except for the front because it needed to be shaved for the drains and the monitors that he needed in his skull. He has an interesting mullet style going on, and it has been a debate on what to do about his hair. We know how much he loved his hair.

So, today he was holding my hand and I said, "Corb do you want a haircut, give me a thumbs up if you do."... Nothing. I asked three times. Then I said, "Corb, if you want to leave your hair long, give me a thumbs up," and the thumb went straight up.

It's incredible to be able to communicate with him on some level. I tell him every day how amazing he is and how proud so many people are of him. I have no doubt that he's going to continue to surprise us.

With a brain injury this severe you have no idea what you're going to get. What's been lost, what will come back, and what won't come back. The brain is so complex. Expressions and emotions are higher functions in the brain, and we didn't know if Corbin would have any of that again. So, to see him playing around with Grace was incredible. That was Corbin showing a little tiny piece of his personality from before the accident.

Having him turning the corners of his mouth up in what looked like a smile was huge for us. The tiny movements like controlling his eyes to follow us, the slightest movements of his mouth, the control of his hand enough to squeeze mine were monumental. It was like a newborn. Every little sound they make, when they finally learn how to control what their hands can do and purposely grab your face is incredible to experience. That's what we lived for, these small improvements that showed us Corbin was still in there.

Corbin's hair was his pride and joy. He loved that hair and had been growing it out for some time. I couldn't imagine what he would have thought if he was awake when they had to shave it. At this point the shaved spots in the front were starting to grow back and the back was getting very long. He had a full-fledged mullet, and I have no problem admitting I wasn't a fan.

I had spoken with Corbin's Aunt Christine who's a hairstylist about cutting it. The first time we talked about it we were in the ICU, and she came in with her scissors. She was going to try to even it out. As soon as we told Corbin what was going on, his blood pressure went up. So, we took that as a sign to wait. By this point the mullet was getting out of control, and I was pushing for a haircut. Once again, Corbin made it very clear what he wanted, despite my best effort to explain what was going on at the top of his head. Getting him to communicate with me was far more important than that the awful hairstyle was.

He was getting stronger by the day. Something definitely turned on in his brain and we could see it in everything he was doing.

Corbin Style - Journal Entry — August 21, 2018

Corbin has had an amazing few days! At this point anything you ask him, he will give you a thumbs up for yes, makes a fist for no, and lays his hand flat for I don't know. He will also lift his hand and wave. Yesterday OT and PT came in and got him sitting up on the side of the bed.

They brought an iPad in and made him reach up to push play to hear the music he likes. He did this all on his own, and then in typical Corbin fashion he gave the "horns" because it was Metallica he chose. The language therapist came in as well and brought a board with letters. She handed Corbin a pen and asked him to spell his name. He pointed to every letter and spelled his name perfectly.

He also started to make more facial expressions. So, without giving all the details, he passed some gas while I was very close to him. I reacted like a mother would, and Corbin giggled and smiled. Apparently, that stuff is always funny to guys of any age. He also was happy to see his dad and gave him big smiles.

We're blown away with how well he's doing and so proud of how hard he's trying. He's the talk of this floor. He's only been here a week and a half, but every nurse that has taken care of him has been coming in to see all the things he's doing.

Spaulding is expecting discharges tomorrow, so it could be as early as tomorrow or Thursday when we move over there.

We were on such a positive stretch. Having communication with Corbin was awesome. It was basic but it was amazing. Every little thing showed us that his brain was working and it felt like it had kicked into high gear. I hadn't got to spend much time with Cohen since the accident. He was with Jeff half the time and my mother the other half. The ICU normally wouldn't let anyone under the age of eighteen stay in the room overnight. They had made an exception for Grace, but Cohen was a definite no.

The tenth floor wasn't as strict. So, on the twentieth of August, Cohen got to spend his first night in the hospital with us. He was so excited; you would have thought that he was in a luxury hotel for the night. He took over Grace's recliner and pulled it right up to Corbin's bed. We picked out movies they both liked, and the brothers were reunited for a short time. Cohen talked to Corbin like nothing was different. He would tell him stories and talk about things they had to do when he got home.

The next day, Cohen was playing with this little orange stress ball he had brought with him, and he put it in Corbin's hand. At this point, Corbin could only lift his left arm a little. He would squeeze your hand or do a few gestures like thumbs up or horns, but that was about it for his body movement. Next thing you know, he pulls his forearm back to his chest and throws it at Cohen. Our mouths dropped!

I grabbed my phone and started videotaping as he did it two more times. Cohen tried a third time. Corbin took his fingers and pushed it away, as if to say, "That's it. I'm done." We were stunned. What the heck just happened? Where did that come from? I knew that was huge. Cohen was so proud of himself! "See Mom. Corbin reacts for me. I should be here every night."

That wasn't Corbin's only major shocker for the day either. After Cohen left, it was just Corbin and me sitting there, when his nurse walked in. She started telling me a story about a patient they called a "frequent flyer." Because of HIPAA, she couldn't tell me much, such as what she was battling or her name. She could only say that this patient had been admitted many times, and she had a motto "It's not a bad life. Just a bad day."

It sounded like maybe it was a mental health situation. She was there at the same time we were, and she had heard about Corbin and his story. She asked Nurse Erica if she would bring us one of the bracelets that she had made with her motto on it. She had been going through her battle for years, and it's what got her through the tough times. She thought it might help us also.

By the end of the story we were both crying. I asked if I could meet her and if the nurse would bring her a Corbin Strong T-shirt and bracelet. We could support each other.

When she left the room, I put my head down on the side of Corbin's bed and cried. I was full of so many emotions. I was touched by her thoughtfulness, her strength, the magnitude of all of it. I succumbed to the challenges of everything we had been going through. I tried to be so strong, and just when you feel like you're going to crumble, you realize it is just a bad day.

As I cried, I suddenly felt a hand on my head almost petting me. The hand then grabbed my shoulder, and I looked up to

Corbin who was crying too. Tears were running down his face. I thought that I must have scared him. I tried to never cry or get emotional in front of him, but I let my guard down and he saw how emotional I was. I wanted everything to be positive, so I sat right up and said, "You're okay, Corbin. You're doing great! I'm not crying because of you!"

His mouth was trying to move, and it looked like he was trying to shake his head no. He kept grabbing my wrist and reaching for the bracelet. I took it right off my wrist and put it on him. I wrapped my arms around him, and we both cried.

He understood everything that was said. My tears turned to joy. He gave me everything I needed that day. He was so brave; he was fighting so hard, and I knew he was coming back to me.

Seven Weeks - Journal Entry — August 22, 2018

So, the new journey begins with therapy at 8 a.m. tomorrow. It's three hours a day and they will push him, but he wants it. He wants to get better. He tells me and you can see the effort he puts in.

Leaving Boston Children's Hospital was very difficult. They are amazing doctors, nurses, support staff, and all-around kind people. I've never met people who genuinely care about my child so much and treat us like family. They are such a huge reason Corbin is where he is, and for that I will forever be grateful for all they have done.

Let's see how much Corbin can keep wowing us all in this next leg of the journey.

The twenty-second started like any other day. Our normal morning routine began when in flew our nurse, Tonna, who screeched, "YOU HAVE A ROOM! YOU'RE MOVING TO SPAULDING TODAY!"

Omg what a shock! Moving? It was exciting and scary. *I have to pack this whole room.* I thought, *I can't believe this is really happening!* I went into the bathroom for a slight emotional breakdown, and then I texted everyone and told them the good news. Paul rushed right down to be with us. I got packing right away, and then we sat and waited.

There was a small communication error, and the person we thought was calling for the required transportation thought another person was doing it. So, we got a later move than expected, but we didn't care. We were breaking out one way or another.

Children's has this great tradition called the Bubble Parade. Once Corbin was all transferred from his bed onto the mobile bed, the EMTs came and had Paul and I go out to the hall. All of the doctors and nurses were lined up with little containers of bubbles. The song "Sunshine in My Pocket" was playing. Harriet, Paul's friend who had checked on us since day one, was also out there to send him off.

They wheeled Corbin out of his room, and hundreds of bubbles started floating around us. Everyone said goodbye and cheered Corbin on. It was surreal. We had been at Children's for fifty days, forty-nine nights, thirty-eight days in ICU. I couldn't believe either of us had made it that far. I couldn't believe that it was actually happening. We did it. We survived the worst of it.

Saying goodbye was bittersweet. We wanted out, but at the same time that had become our home. The doctors and nurses had become our family. We didn't know what to expect at Spaulding. Would the staff take care of him as well, would they be as nice, would I trust them like I trusted these amazing people who kept my son alive? I was apprehensive but we were up for the challenge. I knew Corbin was up for it.

19

AND THEN HE SPOKE

*M*oving fast! - *Journal Entry — August 24, 2018*

We got settled into Spaulding pretty late, and it must have been a lot on Corbin because he didn't sleep much at all the first night. Nurses were in at 7:30 a.m. getting him ready and OT started at 8 a.m. OT is considering casting his right arm for about five days at a time, and then recasting to stretch it out. PT got him a special wheelchair ready so they can get him up to the gym and outside. Speech focused on the trach, taking pressure readings to see about getting a smaller one and eventually getting it taken out.

We met with countless doctors and specialists for the rest of the day. Some of the medication has a slightly sedative effect. So, they want to lower those and eventually put him on some that work to arouse the brain, and hopefully it will help him emerge more. Respiratory works closely with speech, and the therapist came back and said he wanted to switch him to a smaller trach as early as today.

He was in a great mood. He held my hand, so I asked if he wanted to arm wrestle. He smirked and whipped my wrist to the bed. We did that over and over. He was pretty happy with himself.

He FaceTimed with Grayson which made him smile. After that, we looked through pictures and videos on my phone, and every photo with Grayson made him smile or giggle. He's always been such a great big brother.

We used to call him the baby whisperer. Grayson was born when Corbin was fourteen. He wasn't happy about another child at first, but the second he came to the hospital and held that baby, it was all over. Grayson would be fussy, and Corbin would come right over and start walking around with him, swaying back and forth. Grayson would settle right down and fall asleep.

There was just something about Corbin's kind gentle demeanor that put everyone at ease. You couldn't have asked for a better kid. He was kind to everyone. He was a great big brother to all of his siblings.

Finally, about 9 p.m. everyone was done with him, so we sat down to watch a movie. Corb lasted about five minutes, I lasted fifteen. We both slept pretty well, and his first therapy appointment wasn't until nine. So, we got to sleep until eight. At 8:15, respiratory was here, and we changed his trach to a smaller size and capped it. He is now breathing without the trach and can use his voice when he's ready.

This is a huge step. If this goes well, the next step is removing the trach. They move quickly here! OT was next. No word on casting or not yet, but he does have a beanbag brace on the right arm to stretch it out. Corbin's right side doesn't move much and is very tight, so that's really been where all of the OT's focus is going right now.

Speech will be here at eleven and then PT at two. We can't wait to get him in the chair and out and about. I go stir crazy in theses rooms, and I can't imagine poor Corbin who never gets to leave the room, let alone the bed. I'm so excited for him. I think great things are in the works here

Spaulding was no joke. The facility wasn't for the slackers. It was go, go, go, from day one. There wasn't room for taking anything slow. At first, I had a hard time with the pace of things. I thought he was fragile, and they were going right for it. They'd get him out of bed, change his meds, cast his arm, get the trach out, go, go, go. The first few days were a whirlwind. We weren't used to this hectic schedule.

We still managed to get in our relaxation time here and there. He loved seeing pictures of the kids or facetiming with family. It was so much fun to see him smile and giggle. I couldn't wait to have them all back together someday.

Five Days In - Journal Entry — August 27, 2018

It's been five full days at Spaulding now. Corb gets up into his chair, and he leaves the room every day. He doesn't do therapy in his room. He goes to the gym or the speech therapists' room. He is eating ice chips, which he loves, and drinks water out of a spoon. The swallowing tests are very important for getting him to eat real food and taking the trach out. The trach has been capped since Friday with no issues, so it could come out as early as the end of this week!

His left arm moves more every day, and he has started trying to pull out his feeding tube in his nose. I've probably explained it before but the tube in his nose is an NJ tube. It bypasses his stomach and goes right into the intestines to give him his nutrition. He surgically had a feeding tube put in his stomach, but his stomach hasn't been working properly. So, the tube stays open and drains whatever his stomach produces. Even a small kink in that line makes him vomit, although these last few days they have been trying to clamp it on and off, to see if he can tolerate it.

Yesterday, we got up to almost ten hours clamped with no issue.

The goal is to get all feeds and meds through the tube into his stomach. If he continues to tolerate the clamping, they will slowly start to feed him through that and the one in his nose can come out.

I feel awful for him because it's clearly bothering him a lot. He has a brace on the one arm he can move so he doesn't pull it out, and it very clearly upsets him. I keep telling him it's temporary. I took the brace off the other day and he still went for it, so I put a sock on his hand to try to prevent it. He put his hand up to his mouth, bit onto the sock, and pulled his hand out with a smirk on his face. It was so funny.

Yesterday, he got a visit from his sisters and cousin, who is also one of his best friends. It was so awesome to see. They were laughing and joking with him. Corbin was so happy, all smiles and giggles. Laughing at their jokes and goofing around with them. I think that kind of therapy is as important. That stimulation brightens his mood so much.

It's so amazing to see how much he remembers and comprehends. I give him my phone with the pictures open, and he uses his fingers and swipes to the next one. Grace gave him her phone. He opened Snapchat and started picking people, and even took a picture and sent it. Speech comes in and asks him about fifty questions. He answers every one correctly with yes and no hand gestures.

They show him sign language like thank you, I love you, and bathroom. He remembers them all and uses them. But when it comes to his body, his right side barely moves, he's not speaking, and he can't hold his head up. But that's why we're here. I can't help but have really high hopes for him with everything he's showing us. Either way, I remind myself every day how thankful I am that he is still here and how far he has already come.

This week they will probably end up casting his right arm to get it stretched out. Today they will add a medication that is supposed to stimulate his brain more and make him more alert, along with more PT, OT, and speech. Then, his seventeenth birthday is Saturday. At the end of this week, the whole team of doctors and therapist will meet with Dad and I to give us their guesstimates on length of stay, what they think they can do for him, and what changes the house could need for his eventual return.

I assumed Corbin was pretty sick of seeing me day in and day out for almost two months, so visits from family were so welcome. Mari, Grace, and Tanna were together all the time before the accident, so to see them all sit around him making him giggle made my week.

Only one person could stay in Corbin's room with him at Spaulding, so Grace was now staying with my mother. Field hockey had started so her time with Corbin was limited. She begged to not play field hockey so she could get down to see him more, but I wouldn't let her quit. She didn't understand, she needed to keep her life as normal as possible. It wasn't much easier for me though. She had been my constant companion all summer, and I missed her as much as she missed me.

And Then He Spoke . . . Journal Entry — August 30, 2018

It's been a busy few days for all of us. Corb had Dad and Gramma taking care of him while I went home to get the other kids off to their first few days of school.

His Dad updated us that Corbin has started moving his right side more which barely moved before two days ago. He also has had the peg tube in his stomach clamped since Monday night and has tolerated it with no problem. The plan is to start slowly putting his feeds through it so they could get the one in his nose out.

When I checked in this morning, my mother told me that she woke up at 4 a.m. to Corbin laying there with his whole feeding tube in hand playing with it. This means all hydration and nutrition stops. I arrived at around 1:15, and by 1:30 p.m. the ambulance was here to transport us back to BCH for a new feeding tube.

When I got to Corbin's room, he was in his chair getting stretched by OT. He was all smiles and thumbs up when he saw me. I showed him some new movies and a DVD player I got for his room, and he was happy about that as well.

Then he made this sound, and the therapist said, "I just heard your voice, Corbin." So, I started asking him if he wanted to say anything. To be honest, I don't even remember what I asked him, but all of a sudden, he verbally answered me "yes." I started laughing thinking that didn't really happen. He started laughing also, either at me or in disbelief that he actually did it. I had secretly warned him that if he spoke while I was gone, I was going to kick his butt. So, at least he listened.

I guess, as soon as he started to wake up and respond to us, I expected him to eventually talk. No one told me that he would for sure, it was a gut feeling. His eyes had way too much to say for him not to, but that didn't make it any less exciting.

It's like that moment you wait for when you have a baby. What will their first word be? What will their voice sound like? You can't wait to hear it! That's what today felt like. Like hearing his voice for the first time all over again. Knowing that he can physically do it, but also knowing that he can tell us how he's feeling and what he needs.

So that's what I told him. "Corbin now you can tell us if something hurts, I need a drink, I want ice chips . . ." So, then he looked right at me and said, "Yes, I want ice chips." Let me tell you, he got a lot of ice chips tonight.

We didn't get back to his room until around 10:30 tonight. He has a new feeding tube and nice big padded mitts on his hands. Now, he can't pull the tube out while no one is looking. He says it was an accident both *times, and he was itching and hooked it. I'm not so sure that I believe that, but he's very determined to either itch or pull. This is the same determination that has gotten him this far so fast. It's hard to be mad about that.*

I got a picture from his school tonight while we were sitting in the ER, and it brought me to tears. So thoughtful and amazing. Corbin stared at it in awe, just as moved as I was that everyone was thinking of him. As I know he was thinking of them, at what should be the first week of his senior year. Thank you!!

Little did I know what I was in for when I got in his room. Someone was always working on Corbin, so it was no surprise when OT was there when I arrived. Speech had been working on getting him to speak and find his voice, but nothing had happened yet. Then it happened. OMG. His voice was there.

He could speak! It was the most amazing sound and better than his first words as a baby. It was the quietest voice I had ever heard, you had to get close to hear him. After he answered yes to me, he said, "Hi Mom." I practically jumped in his arms, kissing his cheeks! I couldn't even believe it. I was instantly less upset about the feeding tube.

I spent the ambulance ride and the rest of the night trying to get him to say something, anything! God, I missed that voice! I was so worried about never hearing it again. Now that it was back, I couldn't get enough. It was tough at first. Sometimes it didn't make sense. It was like his mouth moved and sound came out, but it wasn't clear words. I didn't care. It was sound, we'll get there with more rest!

The ER visit was long like they always are, and poor Corbin was parched. He hadn't had any liquid or feeds since 4 a.m.. We sat in the room, and he kept trying to sign that he was thirsty.

I was going through every cupboard and drawer trying to find something that I could put a little water in just to wet his mouth.

The tough times weren't so tough anymore. He was hungry and thirsty. We were back at Children's. But he was happy, and I was happy. He spoke today! While we were sitting there watching videos on the phone to pass the time, I got a message with a picture. His entire high school was outside all together holding letters spelling out CORBIN STRONG. This was to be the start of Corbin's senior year, and the entire school was thinking of him and sending their support.

Corbin was in shock, his mouth dropped, and I cried. It meant so much to me, every single bit of support. But now, to get to see Corbin's reactions and how much it meant to him, had also made me very happy.

I don't think anyone who has not been in this kind of position can truly understand the magnitude of these gestures. From a kind word to organizing a school-wide photo to show support, they are game-changers. They keep us going, they give us hope, they give us strength. What can seem like no big deal to the person writing a supportive message, can make all the difference to the recipient.

Thankful - Journal Entry — September 1, 2018

I don't know a better word to describe how I feel. Thankful. Thankful that Corbin is here, and we are celebrating his birthday with him today. Thankful he's doing everything we were told he would probably never do, only eight weeks ago. Thankful for our families, friends, and all of the amazing people who continue to support us and show us so much love.

For those who don't follow Facebook, we had a little surprise birthday party for Corbin today. He's been getting up in his chair every day, and the therapists gave me permission to take him off the floor and outside for the first time today. He thought we were going outside for a walk, but when we came out of the doors a big group of his friends and family were waiting with pictures, banners, and gifts. He was SO happy!

He spent the next few hours goofing off and enjoying his day. It was so great to see how happy it made him. All of it. I showed him every comment/message people left about his birthday, every card, every text, and every video. I'm sure he's never felt so special. He just raises his eyebrows, and his eyes get really big like he can't believe it. He's as taken back by the love and support, and everyone is overjoyed with the progress he's making.

I can't bear to think of what today would have been like without him. So, instead of wishing things were different in any way, I'm thankful we all got to see him smile and enjoy the day. He's here to kiss goodnight. I get to tell him how proud I am of him and how much I love him.

Today was Corbin's seventeenth Birthday. Birthdays were always a big deal in our house. Your birthday was YOUR day. You pick what we do, you pick what we eat, and you pick who's going to be there to do it with you. How do you celebrate a birthday in therapy when you can't leave, you can't eat, and you can't have many people in your room for a party?

You plan ahead and get approval to take him outside without assistance (we practiced without Corbin knowing for this reason). You also get all your amazing family and friends to show up and pull off the best birthday surprise ever. Corbin knew that we couldn't leave. He knew that he couldn't eat cake or pizza, but it was still his birthday. We were still going to celebrate.

Steve had come a few days prior and gave him the best gift he could ever dream of. It was a massive signed matted and framed jersey of Julian Edelman. He was in heaven! Anything with Edelman on it was the way to Corbin's heart.

At the time, Corbin's orally ingested food consisted of ice chips. I asked his speech therapist if I could freeze sweet tea which was Corbin's favorite drink to feed him for his birthday. She agreed and Corbin feasted on crushed sweet tea ice. He acted like it was the best thing he had ever tasted. I couldn't get each spoonful in fast enough.

I had told Jeff what I had planned and that he was welcome to come. I invited his mother also. I didn't know if he would join us seeing as we were planning the party outside of the hospital. Though, soon after I invited him, he asked if Angie could come. I reminded him that there was a court order.

Jeff, his mom, and Cohen showed up that morning to say happy birthday. I asked Jeff if Cohen could stay for the party, as it was Jeff's weekend to have him. He didn't allow Cohen to stay. Unfortunately, Cohen got about a twenty-minute visit before they left. It was never easy dealing with that situation, but he wasn't ruining the day with drama.

Corbin hadn't been outside in months, and I told him I got special permission for his birthday to take him outside for a walk and some fresh air. He was so excited. Once I knew that the party was set up and all the people were outside and ready, I put Corbin's shades on, and we got in the elevator. When we got outside there were about twenty to thirty family members and friends. There were banners, decorations, food, and everyone sang happy birthday to him.

It was amazing! He needed this. To see everyone who loved him cheering him on brought smiles from ear to ear. Our families pulled off the best surprise party ever!

I couldn't have been any happier. My heart was full. To get

one more day, one more smile, one more chance to tell him that I loved him was a gift in itself. To get a birthday that was nearly taken away from us, was more than I could have asked for. I felt like the most blessed person on the planet.

20

THE DREADED FAMILY
MEETING

Progress Continues - Journal Entry — September 4, 2018

    Corbin continues to surprise us all. Monday, he did about eight assisted stands in PT. He held on to the wall. The therapist helped him get up to his feet and kept him stable as he stood. He did so much of the work, and she was impressed with how much he did on his own. Today he was moved from his bed to his chair with help.

    They took him from sitting on the side of the bed instead of being lifted in the sling. It's with plenty of assistance but it's how it all starts. He's putting in hard work, and he loves how it feels to see himself getting there. To feel the possibilities of what he could do.

    The PT was telling him in his first session, which was less than two weeks ago, that he had a hard time following commands and he was slow to understand. Now he does what she says instantly, and he's actively participating and really trying. She's so impressed with what he's done in such a short time. She said with injuries like his, this is beyond impressive progress.

He's also getting louder with his voice. It's such a soft whisper, which is normal when your voice comes back after an injury like this, but he's working hard in speech to be louder. He has to be reminded to use his voice often. He's so used to saying yes and no with his hands that it's hard to remember to speak. He did use his voice enough the other day to tell me which players to pick for week one of fantasy football.

Earlier in the day he was watching football and said something I couldn't quite understand. He said, "Mom it's a name, we need him for our fantasy team." He's so funny. I'm surprised every day with what comes out of his mouth. He's still the easy-going, laid back kid he always was. He still has a goofy sense of humor and all the cravings for the awful junk food he always loved. He's so much the same kid, in just a different way for now.

Another huge step is that he's been getting fluids into his stomach through the feeding tube. The one through his nose has been decreasing, while the one in his stomach has been increasing and he's been tolerating it fine. Hopefully in a day or two he can get that awful thing out of his nose. It drives him crazy, and he has to have the big gloves on his hands twenty-four seven so he can't pull it out.

It's been torture for him! He's so funny because if I take them off for anything, he asks to have them put back on because he knows how much it itches. He knows that he can't help but rub or itch his nose. He doesn't want to go through having a new one put in.

The doctors and therapists have scheduled a meeting for this Thursday to go over what they are predicting for Corbin. How long they think his stay will be, what they see him being able to do by the time he leaves, and so on. It's a mixed bag of feelings. I want to know but it's scary at the same time. I'm sticking with Corbin showing me. He has been nothing short of a miracle till this point and I don't see that slowing down. He's clearly "that kid."

I was a bit gun-shy when it came to family meetings with the hospital staff. Things did not go very well up until that point. I was expecting negativity. I thought Corbin was progressing great, but Spaulding seemed like they were on a different time frame. What if he didn't get better fast enough? What if they were not happy with his progress? I always stressed waiting to hear the news.

I met with the doctors and the social worker from day one to make sure that they were on the same page as Children's with the court order. So, at least, that was one less thing I had to worry about. I did ask Paul to be there with me knowing Jeff wouldn't show up. He didn't come more than once a week, and it wasn't a day he would show up.

Corbin's voice was nothing more than a whisper. I'd often have to get right near his mouth to understand him. That day we had been talking about fantasy football, and we always had sports on the TV. Last year, I got signed up for fantasy football at the restaurant I worked at. I was clueless. I knew the key players on the Patriots but that was the limit of my football knowledge. So, Corbin took over my team, and we came in third!

I never put a thought into it this year until I got an email telling me to make moves to my team. The owner of the restaurant, Doug, knew how much Corbin loved it and signed us up. Corbin still didn't talk all the time. He needed to be reminded. One day, while were talking about our team and what I should do. I said how clueless I was, and he responded.

I tried over and over again to understand him until, finally, I gave him my phone and he typed what he was trying to say. He said, "It's a player and we need him." What the holy hell? He was so with it. He never stopped surprising me! Physically and mentally he was blowing us all away!

Speechless - Journal Entry — September 7, 2018

I often try to think of a cute title for these updates, but today it was hard. I wanted to say "miracle," and then I was thinking something about happy tears or just plain in shock. I'll get to why.

Corb has had some big changes in the last few days. In PT he's still working on standing, and now he's adding taking steps while he's up. The therapists are also not using the lifts and transferring him to the chair from a seated position on the edge of the bed. He is doing so much of the work and getting so strong.

Today the OT was amazed! She was in shock at how well he was doing and couldn't believe it. I realized today that I assumed what they were saying was part of the therapy, and that things like being so positive and encouraging was part of what they do, but I was wrong.

Last night, Corbin decided to pull his NJ tube again. Earlier in the day, I told him it would only be a few more days that it had to stay in, and that I would ask the doctors if they would let him pull it out. It was sort of joke, but it was worth a shot. They took his mitt off to wash him up and left the room to grab some things. I wasn't looking and, the next thing I know, I hear a weird noise. I look and the whole thing was in his hand.

The nurse practitioner came in and gave me the option of going to Children's to put it back in. I said no way! He's done. His full feeds through that tube were 90 ml an hour, and he was already getting 70 ml an hour through his stomach. Even if they wanted to keep it at 70 for a day it was better than torturing him with another tube down through his nose and down his throat. They said okay.

We stuck with the same rate overnight, and by this afternoon he was at full strength through his stomach tube and doing fine. Even all of his meds were going into his stomach for the first time, and he's been doing perfectly well.

Corbin looked like he was wearing boxing gloves, but the doctors referred to them as Mickey Mouse mitts. Those things were the size of boxing gloves, and they were on his hands constantly. I took them off one day to show Jenn the signing he could do. As soon as he did the signs, he put his hands up and asked me to put them back on. He didn't even trust himself with not pulling the tube out. It was making him insane. Even with the gloves, he was constantly rubbing his face.

There was a light at the end of the tunnel though. Feeds through the tube in his stomach were finally being tolerated so the nose tube was on a countdown to be removed. How nice would it be, to free his hands and stop making him crazy? It couldn't come soon enough for Corbin. I let him take the gloves off for a minute when the nurses left, and I told him not to touch it.

I reminded him what it was like getting a new one and going without food and water, and he said he was fine. Two minutes later, I looked up and it was ten inches out of his nose and gripped in his hand. His face said *whoops*. The last time he pulled it out, a nurse tried to push it back down, which is how they often put them in. When I told Rosa about it, she said they should never do that with Corbin with the damage he had.

She said if it ever happens again, pull it all the way out so it can't be pushed back down. So, I said screw it. I knew it was almost all the way out, so I pulled it out and called the nurses in. They were surprised that he got it all the way out. I shrugged and put my hands in the air. So, Corbin and I sneakily did away with the feeding tube that night and everyone slept better.

We were preparing for the long-anticipated family meeting. All of the doctors, nurses, caseworkers, social workers, and therapists planned to sit down and go over what they see for Corbin's future. It's been long-awaited but stressful to think about at the same time.

It started with PT, and they said they think we will need to rent a wheelchair when we get home. "Rent?" I asked.

They answered, "Yes, we feel for long trips or extended periods on his feet, at first, will require it but only temporarily." I was thrilled at that assessment, as this indicated the chair was a short-term need.

Then, they talked about his speech. They believe that the Nj tube going in and out so many times has actually made the vocal cords swollen, and that could have something to do with how quiet he is with his voice. They expect it will fully come back. I asked about flavored ice chips, and they suggested we jump to pureed food. They would try them later in the day at speech therapy.

They said when he first gets home, he will most likely need home tutors, but they expect that he will eventually return to school this year and potentially even graduate. That's where the shock began to kick in. I felt like a mother on school parent's night, expecting the worst and learning the teachers actually think your kid is awesome.

Next, they said they don't foresee any major home modifications needed. That's where my confusion started. I said that he needs to go up five stairs to get in the house, and his bedroom is down a full flight from there. They said worse case he will need a first-floor bedroom temporarily.

I asked about a handicap bathroom for the wheelchair. They said he should be walking with a walker or cane, or maybe even nothing by the beginning of October. That's when the *what the heck is going on* kicked in. Am I hearing things? Am I missing something? I mean he's kicking butt and he's progressing unbelievably fast, but what I'm hearing shocked me beyond my wildest dreams.

They said that Corbin is going to walk out of here. It could be with a cane or a walker for now, but they believe that's just temporary. I asked about a special vehicle. They said nope, he should be able to ride in anyone's car.

It was the most unreal news. We have been on Cloud Nine all day. He could graduate, he could WALK back into school. They see endless possibilities for Corbin, and less than two-and-a-half months ago they told us to say goodbye.

Continues to Impress - Journal Entry — September 7, 2018

As if yesterday's news wasn't the most amazing feeling, today was even more incredible, as he just continues to push the progress to unbelievable levels.

In PT he practiced standing and only needed one therapist to assist because he was doing so much of the work himself. His upper body was more slouched over on Monday, but today he was barely being supported and was standing up straight. Then, they decided to try walking. He walked about three to four feet, four different times. Then, he went to the gym and used a peddle bike for five minutes straight. He was stopped to rest and then asked, "Can you hit the continue button?" The therapist said, "Wow, I think you're the first patient that has asked to keep going." So, he continued to pedal for another ten minutes.

He knows what he wants and he's going to work hard for it! He also brushed his teeth and fed himself today. It's amazing to see him without being hooked up to all the monitors and IVs. The only thing that he's hooked up to is the stomach feeds. It's such a relief when I think about where he came from.

Speaking of his stomach, they continue to go up on the amount he's getting so that he can be off it for more hours a day. The goal is to feed him larger amounts over shorter periods. It's sort of like how we normally eat meals, and then as the intake of regular food goes up, the stomach feeds can come back down.

Tonight, he told me he was bored. So, we got him up in the chair, and we went outside for a walk. As I was pushing him around, I couldn't help but think about being on the brain injury floor today where he went to use the bike. Everyone we encountered in the gym, or even that we heard walking through the halls, had such severe brain injuries, the type of injuries I was preparing myself for. They weren't communicating like Corbin, they weren't aware, or even in control of their bodies or actions. It was heartbreaking, and I couldn't help but feel so blessed that's not what Corbin is dealing with.

I stopped pushing him and asked if he remembered being there today and what he saw and heard. I explained all of those people had severe brain injuries like him. I reminded him of what the doctors said yesterday about his recovery. I told him how lucky he was, how lucky I was. He said, "Oh trust me, I know!"

How lucky we are that his treatments have been at the #1 pediatric hospital and the #2 rehab facility in the country. What a beautiful place to be if you have to be stuck somewhere.

21

SO THANKFUL TO BE ALIVE

lowing my mind - Journal Entry — September 10, 2018

    Corbin had a pretty easy-going weekend. He went off of a few medications and down on others. He also went up on his feeds so that now he's getting his nutrition over hour-and-a-half spans at mealtimes, instead of constantly running. This give us much more time to be outside or, at least, out of the room.

    Corbin was very excited for football this Sunday and very proud that his picks for our fantasy team did so well. He had some visitors to watch the game with, which always makes him smile as well.

    Today, he decided to blow us all away and walk with minimal assistance. He did it a few times and kept having to be told to slow down because he wanted to go. He gets stronger every day. The look on his face is priceless. He is so proud of himself, and he tells me how good it makes him feel to be doing all of this. This kid is blowing my mind.

    Corbin had an X-ray Saturday in hopes of clearing his spine so he can get the neck brace off. The doctors came back and said his spine looked perfect. Like a normal spine. After many breaks that is. They still needed to get it cleared by the surgeon at BCH, but they were feeling good about what they saw. After I left this afternoon, Corbin's Auntie Christine, who is staying with him tonight, texted me and said the neck brace is gone!!

One more step in the right direction. It will be much more comfortable for him. He will get to strengthen his neck muscles, and he will be able to get his head in a better position for eating and swallowing.

I also wanted to take a minute to thank Grace's coaches and field hockey team for getting special team Corbin shirts made to support us! We LOVE these pictures and are so grateful for how much they have done during all of this. You guys are the best.

Busy week - Journal Entry — September 15, 2018

Corbin has had a busy week. It started with the brace being taken off, which he is doing amazingly well with. His muscles are tight and sore, but he's holding his head up very well. Better every day.

He has started getting daily meals now. It started with lunch and dinner and tomorrow he'll be getting breakfast as well. It's all puree right now, which I am so surprised that he's eating so well. He' been a very picky eater his whole life, and the food options are not really anything he would have eaten before. Except for the mashed potatoes. He's a big fan of those! He tries everything and is eating so much, that it's enough to replace some of his daily tube feedings.

Starting tomorrow they are going to start counting the calories he's taking in from his meals, and if it's enough, tube feedings will be discontinued. It will probably take a week, but such huge progress. He's so ready for Taco Bell and buffalo tenders, and he knows this puree is the first step to get there. So, even though it's not what he wants, he still does it.

Corbin has been working very hard in therapy. He walked forty feet this week and is no longer using the lift at all to be transferred. He actually holds himself up really well once he's in the sitting position, and then he stands up and pivots into his chair. He loves being outside, so we try to do that as much as possible. Last night, we were walking around the grounds and saw a baby bunny munching away.

I think the biggest changes in Corb this week are cognitive thought. He always sits and doesn't really speak unless spoken to, and this week he started conversations. He asked questions, and he told us when he was uncomfortable or wanted to move. He was a chatterbox today! His voice is still a whisper, but I've heard it come through at a normal level a few times. When he hears it, it becomes even more of a whisper almost like he's afraid of it.

We spent most of today talking. We talked about the accident and his journey since then. We have talked about it before, but today he asked a lot of questions and he wanted more details. He wanted to see pictures of himself and hear about the different surgeries. He's so thankful. I mean not a "wow, I'm a lucky kid," but deeply thankful to be here and so excited to keep working hard and progressing.

He's always been a sweet, polite kid. Though, I think with knowing how lucky he is and how everyone is here to help him get better, he lets everyone know he appreciates what they're doing. He asked me to call the nurse back in today so he could thank her for bringing him his lunch. He's incredible. I told him that he has so many people that think he's incredible, and they can't wait to see all this progress he keeps making.

This kid amazes everyone with his positive attitude and constant smile. He tries his hardest with whatever they ask him to do. He never once complains about any of it. The other night I asked why he had such a big smile on his face, and he said, "Because I'm so happy mom. I'm happy to be alive, and I'm happy to be able to talk." Oh, my heart.

Week Eleven - Journal Entry — September 20, 2018

Yesterday marked eleven weeks since the accident. Some days it feels like it was only yesterday. Some days it feels like it was two years ago but in reality, eleven weeks is a blink of an eye. We were told we could be at Children's for more than six months and then rehab, and here we are eleven weeks later with a rehab discharge date of October tenth. Granted that could be extended, but, most likely, not by more than a week or two. It's absolutely incredible how far he has come in such a short time.

Corb has had a few ups and downs this week. Monday night he was given antibiotics for an infected finger, and he had an allergic reaction. He spent fourteen hours vomiting with an elevated heart rate. He couldn't keep anything down so all food/feeds were stopped, and he was put on IV fluids.

He couldn't do any therapy Tuesday, stayed in bed to rest. But, boy does he bounce back. As soon as he felt better, he started eating again. He went from puree to soft food and is eating so well that all tube feeds have been discontinued. Even his meds are being crushed up and given in yogurt. So hopefully the last tube in him will be out soon!

Yesterday his full voice came back. No more whisper. It's a clear Corbin voice again. He is a chatterbox. He speaks in full sentences, and he's very happy about not having to keep repeating himself because people can't hear him.

Today he decided to kick the walking up a notch. He did a lap and a half around the floor with a one-handed walker and a very small amount of assistance from the PT. It was about 320'.

We all know he still has a long way to go. He will still be in therapy three days a week for a long time when we go home, but he also knows how far he's come and how fast it's happened, and that gives him motivation. We were talking to him today about that and he said, "It's my willpower. It's what I want, so I do it." He'll never stop amazing me.

Sounds Like a Plan - Journal Entry — September 27, 2018

Corbin continues to stay super positive through everything. No matter what they tell him that he's going to try to do or what changes they are going to make, he says, "Sounds like a plan."

Every day he continues to improve. Last week, he was walking with a walker, and this week the walker is gone. He is walking with the support of his therapist's arm around him. He is walking laps around the floor without a break. Today, I was cleared to walk with him out of PT so we can keep working on his stamina. He also started stairs today.

At first, it was up one step then down. Then, it was up five, turn around, and then walk down. He has the strength so it's just practice to get the coordination back. This brain injury really affects every aspect of everything about him. The simplest things for us, take so much more work for him, but he hasn't gotten frustrated once. He wants to keep trying.

Corbin is really enjoying food much more lately! He's been upgraded to soft food, so he eats omelets, French toast, mac and cheese, and even pizza. I took some requests this week while I was home, and he wanted cider donuts from Carter Hill and pizza from Chiefs. Today, he was asking for Doritos. So, his speech therapist let him try some, and she said they will do it again tomorrow. If he does okay, he'll be cleared to have them whenever he wants. Very exciting news for Corbin!

The hospital tries to do some excursions to get the patients out of the building, so yesterday Corb went apple picking. He had a great time and was so proud of himself because he got out of the chair and walked around the tree to pick apples. Uneven ground and all.

Medically he's making gains as well. He has gotten a shot every day since the beginning to prevent blood clots, and he's up walking so much that they have discontinued that. He is getting nothing through his feeding tube, so they have put a call into BCH to see about having that removed.

His med list is constantly shrinking. What he does have left, he is taking by mouth, even swallowing pills. They have moved his discharge date out to October 24th. He is making such great gains with the daily therapy that they think he would benefit from a few more weeks.

He has been confused often lately. He will tell me that he has to work tonight or he dropped someone off. Tonight, he told me we were in Florida. The doctors say it's very common with this type of brain injury, and it won't last. It was scary at first and felt like the first set back that we've had in a while. At first, I would tell him, "No, you're in the hospital you don't have to work." He would argue, but now it's like he gets the thought. But when you tell him, "No Corb we're in Boston not Florida." He thinks about it for a minute and says, "Oh yeah."

I couldn't help but think of the day the accident happened as I was watching him walk the halls with such ease today. I remember thinking he has to survive. No matter what state he's in I'll take him. I'll figure it out. To see him walking today reminded me how far he's come and how he's already surpassed every expectation that the doctors had for him in less than four months. I know the possibilities are endless for this kid.

20 DAYS - Journal Entry — October 4, 2018

Things at Spaulding are still moving forward. In PT, Corbin is working on his endurance walking. Today he did a test to see how far he could walk in six minutes. He did great. Only rested for about thirty seconds. He's also mastering the stairs. They're getting easier and tomorrow they are going to try a full flight. He's sitting himself up in bed much easier, he walks to all of his therapy sessions, and moves around his room with so such ease.

He's rarely in bed now. He sits up in normal chairs, and they are talking about maybe trying to eliminate his wheelchair by the end of next week. He needs someone with him for a little help with balance, but it continues to improve every day.

OT is working hard on his right arm and hand. He still doesn't have much use with the right hand, but it is improving. He's using an arm bike and all kinds of tools to strengthen, stretch, and improve his fine motor skills. Today, he wore a glove that was connected to a tablet that had a program similar to Guitar Hero. He would have to touch the tips of his fingers to the tip of his thumb on cue. It was fun to watch because it was obvious, he wasn't working on his hand physically but it was working on his concentration and cognition. It's pretty amazing to see all of the tools they use.

In speech, he was cleared for regular liquids today, so no more thickening everything. Tomorrow's request is a blueberry hot coffee. Speech works on so many things with him. They do all the testing and retraining for eating and drinking, they work on writing, math problems, reading, and a lot with his memory. His memory is the biggest struggle right now. It started with once or twice a day that he would say something that didn't make sense. Now, it's all the time, every day.

He often thinks he's in Florida, he asks if I grabbed the room key when we leave the room, he thinks he saw someone he hasn't seen in weeks, or he can't remember what he ate earlier in the day. It feels like talking to someone with Alzheimer's. He also starts to get frustrated when I tell him he can't get in his truck that he thinks is parked outside and drive home. Or anything else he thinks is reality and I try to correct him on it.

It has felt like a huge setback because when he first started talking, it was like he woke up. He was "with it," and it was hard to understand why in my feelings like he was regressing. The doctors say it's very normal, and it should get better in time as his brain heals. As hard as it is to watch him struggle with this confusion, I remind myself that he is so much better *than we were prepared for him to be. It's still only been three months! The brain takes years to heal, and this will also be temporary.*

Today is national taco day, apparently, so in honor of that I felt like it was time for Corb to get his Taco Bell. I had a big bag of all his favorites delivered, and he couldn't have been happier. I don't know how he ate as much as he did but he kept going. Every day he keeps getting closer and closer to getting back to his normal. He talks about going home every day, and we're all so ready to take him back there. Twenty DAYS!!

The confusion was getting worse and it was starting to wear on Corbin. It was like a juggling act to keep him in the know or ride it out. He always talked about going home, wanting to be home, and sometimes he would tell me he wasn't listening to the doctors anymore. He believed he was going to get in his truck and drive home. Instead of arguing, I'd say, "Okay, let's go for a walk, and you can show me where the truck is." By the time we got outside, he didn't remember why we were even going outside. The problem was solved, and then we'd go for a nice walk around the water.

Trying to live life in two different places was difficult. I was now spending two nights a week at home with the other three kids and the rest of the week with Corbin. I was in frequent contact with Brenda throughout this journey. Like so many, she wanted to do whatever she could to help. Knowing Corbin was coming home and that we had to convert a first-floor room into a new bedroom for Corbin, she asked if she could help. I jumped all over it.

I didn't know how I was going to pull it off in the two days a week that I was home. I was here, and I knew she would make it special and amazing. Around the same time, she and my mother spoke and decided to do a whole first floor makeover. They wanted us to come home to something incredible.

We had the same living room furniture for ten years, and the rest of the first floor was a project in the making. All great ideas but half-finished projects with not enough time to complete any of them. I was told to pick out the couch and a lift chair for Corbin, and they said the rest was in their hands. It was going to make coming home all that much more special.

The Mullet is Gone - Journal Entry — October 12, 2018

Corbin has been very busy! He is walking around everywhere. We only use his chair when we leave the hospital. He's working on his endurance, building muscles, walks up and down full flights of stairs, and has even practiced getting in and out of a car.

I made a post on Facebook last week of Corbin walking down a hall sideways while tossing and catching a ball. It was less than two months ago when he was nonverbal, and the only part of his body he was moving on his own was his left arm from his elbow down. He tossed a ball to his little brother.

They went back and forth a few times. His trauma doctor told me how amazing it was that he could do this and how much brainpower it takes to do that. Less than two months after being presumed dead, he's walking without assistance, walking sideways while multi-tasking, walking flights of stairs, he writes, he spells, he communicates. If I wasn't watching it with my own eyes, I might not believe it. He's been nothing short of incredible.

His short-term memory is still a challenge, so speech is working on strategies to make that better. They have moved him to a regular diet so he's free to eat or drink anything he wants. I think this will be huge for him to put on weight and muscle. He's eating so much more.

Corb has been on quite a few outings this week. We walked to Dunkin's for coffee on Tuesday. This was the first time walking off the hospital grounds and having to figure out how to navigate the roads. Thursday night, Spaulding organized a Boston Bruins game. We sat in Patrice Bergeron's suite and were escorted down to meet him after. Corb couldn't have been more excited!

Today Corbin had an appointment at Mass General to have his finger looked at. His index finger has been swollen for weeks so it was time for a specialist to look at it. They also believed we were ready for an outing with the car, so they let me load him up and drive him to the appointment. We found our way over and Corb felt like he was escaping.

It turns out there were small shards of glass under the skin. It looked like a very painful procedure, and he did get a lot of glass out. It's crazy the things that seem so minor now, with the amount of major we've been dealing with.

The doctors have decided to keep Corbin one more week, so his new discharge date is 11/1. They would like him there until he's less confused and able to use the bathroom on his own. They believe a little more time with the intense therapy schedule will get him there.

And to end the week, Corbin finally got a haircut!! Anyone who knows Corb knows how attached he is to his hair, so this has been an ongoing battle since he woke up. He finally gave in, so his Auntie Christine came down tonight and it's gone! He's really liking the new style as much as he fought it. THE MULLET IS GONE!!!

At this point, Corbin still wears what is called a condom catheter at night. It is exactly what it sounds like, a condom that is glued on with a tube at the end that goes to the urine collection bag. One of the big concerns with going home is getting him continent so we don't have to use these anymore. During the day it comes off, and we are basically potty training.

He is training his brain again when it's time to go. He doesn't have the sensation to go. So, we get him to the bathroom every hour, sometimes more, because he will think he feels like he has to and then he'll say, "False alarm." Even in the most humiliating times he has a sense of humor. No teenage boy, never mind a seventeen-year-old, wants his mother doing what I had to do. He would say, "I feel as bad for you, Mom."

Most importantly, Corbin got a haircut that week. I had been trying for months to get it cut, but it was ultimately up to Corbin, and the second he agreed I set it up! Auntie Christine and Uncle Scott made the trip down, and we had a blast. Visiting hours were only until 8 p.m. since we were on a pediatric floor, but we weren't quiet that night. Lots of laughing. The nurse heard the laughter, peeked in, smiled, shut the door, and let us enjoy ourselves.

Corbin looked like a different person! The mullet drove me crazy, and it was finally gone! In true "Corbin style," he wanted to save his hair to scare his sister with. So, Christine cut it off in two little pigtails and we put it in a to-go soup container for future entertainment.

22

THERE'S NO PLACE LIKE HOME

The Countdown is Back On - Journal Entry — October 17, 2018

I believe the first of November will be Corbin's discharge date. It's about two weeks out and the whole team believes it won't change. We are now starting to look at outpatient rehabilitation in NH because he will still be getting all three therapies two to three times a week and receiving tutoring at home for now.

Corbin continues to make progress every day. It's really quite amazing, to leave for a day or two and come back to witness major changes. The confusion seems to be getting better. He's asking more questions, notices things, and wants to talk all the time. Some days it seems like it's gone and, other days, it only returns when he's really tired. His short-term memory is the same way. He continues to have the same kind, easy-going attitude about everything, and the hair cut has been a HUGE hit with everyone.

Corbin's strength and endurance increase every day. We don't use the wheelchair at the hospital at all. He went for another walk today to get used to uneven ground and following safety guidelines with crosswalks. In class, he's stepping over obstacles and standing on a balance ball. They are really pushing him right now. They usually schedule an hour of each therapy a day but, some days, he has more than four hours of therapy right now.

Next week, he will be back at Mass General to get the G-tube out. It will be the last tube to finally be removed. He will also get X-rays of his spine while he's there. He has some curving going on at the top that they want to check on. Apparently, with injuries like this, scoliosis can form so they want to make sure it's muscular and not the bones.

Corb is so ready to go home. He tells me every day and is counting the days. He misses everyone so much, wants some normalcy and to be able to do things like go to the movies. When I know more, I'll post it, but I have been told that fire, rescue, and police want to be involved with a welcome home for him. Corb says, "I've never had my own parade." He's very excited!!

He is "that kid." It's unreal what he has accomplished in such a short time. We're all so proud of him. His attitude, his spirit, his drive, and his kind disposition are something to behold.

I remember when he was unconscious for weeks. I would try to find this little spot on his forehead between all of the tubes and wires so I could give him a kiss, and now he can stand up on his own to give me a hug. He doesn't give me one hug that I take for granted.

My spot I would call it. In ICU, Corbin had tubes coming from everywhere. Trying to find another spot to kiss him instead of just his hand was hard, but it didn't stop me from searching one out. If I snuck in between the two towers of machines, monitors, and pumps at the top of his bed, I could safely get between the two monitors that were in his skull and kiss his forehead. That was my spot. I didn't leave his side without kissing his forehead.

Some days, I would sit there with my arms resting on either side of his head, resting my forehead in his, telling him how much I needed him. Now he's standing on his own, right beside me, giving me a hug. It is unbelievable. There is no better feeling.

It's like that moment you get to see and hold your baby for the first time, but times a million. You've held that baby, you've nursed that baby, you've wiped that baby's tears, you've taught that baby, you've given that baby wings to be his own person, and then that baby gets ripped away from you. You watch all the struggle and all the pain. Then you know he's back and, no matter what, it's going to be okay the second he can wrap his arms around you.

ONE WEEK - Journal Entry — October 25, 2018

Spaulding has been pushing Corbin, getting the most out of his last few days. He's getting extra therapy every day on top of education testing. His schedule exhausts me.

Corbin's been doing a lot more outings trying to get acclimated to "out of hospital" life. There have been walks to Dunkin's for his blueberry coffee and a few road trips for doctors' appointments at other hospitals, including this past Monday when he got his feeding tube removed from his stomach. It hasn't been used for a long time, but it requires a surgical procedure to remove it so it was put off a little. Finally, everything has been removed.

He also had X-rays of his spine while he was there, and there are two curves in his spine that they're concerned about. It could be scoliosis that's formed, could be broken bones that have healed wrong, or it could be muscles or lack thereof. He'll see a specialist at Boston Children's Hospital in a few weeks.

The good news is that we will be leaving Spaulding with no equipment except a shower chair and even that is only temporary. His endurance has improved so much. We went to the Museum of Science today, rode in Spaulding's van with no wheelchair, walked around the museum, and up and down stairs. He didn't sit to rest, even once, and that was after having his first therapy at 7 a.m. To think less than a month ago, I was in disbelief when they told me that he would walk out of here.

One week from now Corbin will be home. It's hard to put into words what that feels like. It's impossible to think about him walking out of here without getting emotional. This is a day that I spent a long time wondering if it would ever happen. In one way, it feels like a relief to the end to the most difficult chapter of our lives. In another, this is a new beginning. A beginning to a very different life, filled with multiple appointments every day, but a life I couldn't be more thankful for.

It's a little scary as well. The other day, I compared it to taking him home from the hospital when he was a baby. I was petrified. There are many similarities to taking him home this time also. Granted I have seventeen years of experience this time, but this is a whole new experience. We'll both need some time adjusting to "out of hospital" living but we couldn't be more excited!

We are planning a little welcome home celebration, potentiality with police, fire, and rescue escorts. We've been asked to do a drive through his elementary school so the kids can come out and wave hello and we could be doing the same at his high school before we head home. We will be coming through Boscawen around 12:15–12:30. So, check out Corbin's website or the Team Corbin Facebook page to find out more details about setting up a spot for anyone who wants to see his escort home.

It was so thrilling to think about leaving. Thrilling and scary. Corbin was on so many medications given to him three to four times a day, he was walking but, still a little unstable, so he needed assistance with stairs or uneven ground, and I was still assisting him with dressing, toileting, and showering. He basically required more attention than a toddler. Then there was this new schedule of therapy appointments, a new primary care doctor, all the follow-ups he'd need in Boston. And lastly, not having a doctor at your disposal to check in a few times a day to make sure everything was okay. I knew it was all going to be in my hands now, and I was definitely worried.

It was going to be a whole new life for the kids and me. There were so many uncertainties. Would I be able to manage the new schedule along with the other three kid's schedules, and how was I going to work to support us?

I had so many worries. What if Corbin got confused and tried to get in his truck and drive, or if he went outside in the cold and locked himself out in the middle of the night when I was upstairs? I had a security system put in on the doors and windows that would alert me if any opened after I put him to bed. His bedroom had been moved to the first floor so he had no steps or stairs to get to the kitchen or bathroom, but his old room was in the basement and I worried he might try to go down there.

It all scared me, but that didn't stop the pure joy of knowing I was going to have my whole family all together under one roof again. To spend so long living with all the uncertainty, made this a welcome relief. Don't get me wrong, we still had plenty of it but Corbin coming home, walking out of rehab, and blowing everyone's mind with his miraculous recovery was certain now!

Everyone wanted to be a part of Corbin's homecoming. Luckily, Paul was always such a huge help by filtering all of that kind of stuff for me. I would get messages from the news station or the local paper, and he would respond to them all. We had developed quite a large following with all the updates, and people wanted to make Corbin's homecoming special. Corbin's elementary school, middle school, and high school all wanted us to drive through and were going to get students outside to wave to him and welcome him home.

Paul was doing all the corresponding and setting it all up. It was a great feeling and most importantly we knew how much it would mean to Corbin to finally see how much people really cared about him and have been supporting him through all of this.

We're HOME!!! - Journal Entry — November 2, 2018

There are really no words or not enough words to express the gratitude I have. We are so lucky to be a part of this amazing community!! I never imaged when I started writing these updates that they would be read by anyone other than our families and friends. It started as a way to keep everyone who was worried about Corbin updated. I needed to get my point across that there were no ill feelings involved and for everyone to pull together instead of blaming or bullying. But it's turned into so much more.

I found it was therapeutic for me to write about Corbin, but then when I started getting all the kind words of love and support it gave me strength. I truly believe it gave Corbin strength also because I read him every comment and every message even when he was unconscious. I hope yesterday felt like it was as much of a celebration for you as it was for me because you all helped get Corbin home.

Like I've said before, I wish I could individually thank each and every one of you who said a prayer, wrote us a kind message, took care of our animals, came to Corbin's fundraisers, took care of my other children, and got our home ready for Corbin to come back to. The list is endless for everything all of you have done, and I am SO grateful for all of it.

I saw a sign the other day that said, "Difficult roads often lead to beautiful destinations." It seemed so fitting. I wouldn't have chosen this road, but we're here and we're doing our best. We are positive about the future and thankful for what we have gained along the way. New friends, mended relationships, and more support and love than we could have ever imagined.

We still have a long ride ahead of us, but the biggest hurdles are behind us. Our first night home was perfect, and it was amazing to wake up with everyone under one roof for the first time in what feels like forever. We're planning on a quiet weekend at home, taking a break before therapy in Manchester starts again next week. We'll still be in Boston a few times a month for follow-ups, but right now we're thankful to all be together.

Halloween was upon us, and boy I was so torn. I had Grayson at home, and Cohen was in prime trick or treat age. Then I had Corbin. It was his last night in Spaulding and a big day around there. Even though he was seventeen everyone from the pediatric floor dressed up if they were able to and went around to all the other floors trick or treating. Corbin loved Halloween. He still came with me every year to take the little kids, and this year he got to dress up.

Auntie Christine got him a full-size taco costume, and he was going as his favorite food. I didn't know what to do, but lucky for me Paul was once again there to help me. He came and stayed with Corbin so I could take the little ones and make sure everything was ready at home before Corbin got there. Paul sent lots of pictures of Corbin and the other kids having a great time and collecting lots of awesome gifts. Spaulding really knows how to make kids feel special.

It was a perfect night for all, the little and big kids all had a great time. I think every emotion known to man hit me that night, so sleep didn't really happen for mom.

We got up early the next morning and loaded up the car for our last trip for Spaulding. I was so anxious, the reality of the last few months and what our new reality was, had hit me. When we got to Spaulding, Corbin was up and ready to go. He was so excited to "be free," be home, see friends, just go for a ride in the car, and feel some normalcy.

The line of doctors' forms started piling up, and I signed away while everyone else loaded the last of our things into the car. It didn't feel real. I couldn't believe he was mine again, that he was really coming home. He wasn't just coming home; he was walking out of there only 121 days after I was told to say goodbye to him. What a miracle.

Paul had gotten a GoPro camera for my car so he could record Corbin as he got to see all of the people at his schools and on the way home. He also had one set up in his car so he could follow us and record everything Corbin was seeing. I wasn't quite sure what he had in store for us at that point, but we got in the car and started our journey home. I have to admit I wasn't expecting a ton of people to be outside as it was a really cold and rainy day.

Spaulding was about an hour and a half from our home. About an hour into the trip, we were approaching the toll booths. Paul called and said to go slow through the toll and get behind the state trooper that was waiting there. That was pretty surprising. A state trooper that far from our town to escort us? But that's where our escort started.

From there, we got to the overpass right before our exit, and people were lined up on the bridge with signs, beeping horns and waving. Off the exit we stopped at the rest stop where it was packed! People, signs, tents, food, the media, you name it! We never got out of the car, we just slowly drove through while Corbin had his window down saying hello.

People were saying, "I love you." "I'm proud of you." "You did it, Corbin." "You're 'that kid,' Corbin." I saw people with tears in their eyes as they saw him.

We got in the line with police, fire, rescue, family, even the tow truck company that had towed Corbin's truck for us after the accident and headed for his high school. At the entrance, the school sign was for Corbin, and when we pulled around the corner every high school student had lined up around the school to welcome Corbin home. I use the word incredible a lot, but it was incredible.

After everything he had been through, this was so special for him. Corbin wasn't a star athlete or class president. He was your average high school student who usually blended in with everyone else, but not anymore. He was a rock star. All of these people knew who he was, the fighter, the survivor, and they were all there to support him.

From there, we went through the middle school and it was the same greeting there. They handed us signs and even flowers from one of my teachers when I was a student there.

We were blown away. When we left the first two schools and headed toward the elementary school, we noticed all the people on the side of the road standing in the rain. Businesses had all changed their signs to welcome home Corbin. It was awesome to see how happy all of this made him.

When we got to the elementary school it was the same

welcome. Corbin and Grace both went to that school, and Cohen was still a student there. All of the kids were outside. So many of the classes had spent time making huge signs welcoming him home. Cohen definitely enjoyed the celebrity status, waving to all of his friends and teachers. The rest of the ride home was filled with people outside with signs waving, wanting to get a chance to show their support in person for Corbin. It wasn't until our street and all of the people and signs of our neighbors, that it really hit me. One more bend around the corner and my son would be home. I broke down.

It's the most incredible feeling to know so many people care that much about your child. As parents, we would do anything for our children but to have a whole community, town, city, police departments, fire departments, rescue departments, business, friends, family, and complete strangers care so much about your child is enough to make your heart burst. It was everything I could have ever asked for and it was finally real.

Mostly everyone in the lineup came to the house to see Corbin. The local news station was there recording it all. Everyone wanted to shake his hand or give him a hug, and Corbin got a chance to say thank you.

Once it was family left, we got to bring Corbin inside and give him a tour of the newly made-over house. Brenda had pulled off a miracle! From painted walls and cupboards to the most amazing sports-themed room for Corbin. It had all of his memorabilia people had collected or gifted him while he was in the hospital on the walls, new doors put up for privacy, and a normal bed but with a lift frame so he could still sit in bed like his bed in the hospital. It was amazing! Corbin walked around with his jaw dropped. "I don't even recognize it," he said.

It was such a special day. We got Corbin's favorite pizza, all of his friends showed up, and Corbin was surrounded by all his family as we celebrated the day that we couldn't even imagine a short few months ago. Mission accomplished!

Our new lives began on November 1st. We were so grateful to all be together again, and we're gradually adding daily to our new normal.

Corbin's first therapy visit was scheduled for November 6th, which happened to also be my birthday, celebrating forty-one years.

The day started out pretty normal. Corbin would always get up and head straight for the bathroom. I was sitting at the counter when he came out of his room, gave me a quick hug and a happy birthday before going to the bathroom. When he came out, I heard the door but didn't look. Next thing I know, I hear "Mooommm" in this slow fading voice. I looked over and his eyes rolled into the back of his head.

He fell against the wall and started to collapse. Oh my god, how could this be happening? I flew from my seat and caught his head before it hit the floor. Cohen happened to be home from school that day and he came running. I told him to call 911. I didn't know what happened to Corbin. A seizure, fainting, an aneurysm? His eyes seemed to be rolling, his body was limp, and he was slightly shaking. He was in this state for about a minute.

Just as quickly, he snapped out of it and was waking up. He didn't know what happened. We sat on the floor for a few minutes, and then he tried to stand up. He was only up for a minute or two before he started to collapse again. I remained on the phone with 911 while Cohen called my mother to stay with him and Grayson. He also called Paul to meet us at the hospital.

I managed to get Corbin in a chair where he seemed to be pretty stable until the EMTs arrived. They quickly loaded him into the ambulance as my mother was arriving. They assured me his vitals were fine and to get things settled with the other kids inside. I could then follow them.

The next thing I knew, I looked outside, and the ambulance was stuck in my field. The EMTs were outside trying to dig the tires out. I had to laugh. How does this happen? I went out to the field and offered some of my country living advice on getting out of the mud. They kindly asked if I wanted to get in with Corbin while they worked, so I did.

Corbin was feeling better, sitting up, completely alert, and staying warm in his stuck hospital escort. We laughed when I got in. It was reassuring to see that he was fine, and we weren't in a dire emergency situation. They had called for Concord Rescue to come to rescue Corbin from the mud, so we were waiting for the second ambulance to show up. The arrival of either that or the town backhoe that was also called to pull the ambulance out would solve the immediate issue.

Of course, they showed up at the same time. So, as I was filling out forms for Concord, the massive backhoe got the ambulance out and Concord is no longer needed. Corbin's muddy ride finally begins his journey to the hospital. I couldn't make this up if I tried. It was a birthday I will never forget.

The fainting got worse before it got better. Corbin had MRIs, EKGs, wore an around-the-clock heart monitor and saw every specialist we could find. After every test, it was determined to be common in teenagers and he would outgrow it. It lasted for about three months and then went away.

We had a lot of bumps in the road the first few months, lots of medication changes, side effects, ups and downs with cognition and memory, and exhaustion. We also had this newfound appreciation for the day to day normalcy we took for granted before. Our life wasn't easy. I couldn't work. Corbin needed twenty-four-hour adult supervision and being the only parent in his life, that completely fell on me.

We were all adjusting to the new Corbin. The Corbin who might ask the same question every five minutes, who needed assistance with the same things Grayson did, from bathing to food, to dressing. We even needed to adapt to the freedom we didn't have. These changes were so minute in comparison to what we had previously envisioned that life might be like. It's so easy to paint a pretty picture because none of the adjustments were our driving force. Having Corbin there, happy, functioning better than we could have ever dreamed of, made everything else seem so minor.

23

FINAL THOUGHTS FROM A LOVING MOTHER

I have been asked so many times how I made it through this, and my answer is, how could you not? It was never about me; it was about keeping Corbin alive. When the surgeon and neurologist first came to us after his first surgery and said to say goodbye, something took over.

Maybe, it was deep maternal instinct. Maybe it was a delusional denial but, either way, as soon as I heard the words "you need to say goodbye," a switch went off and a wall went up. It was a mission to make sure that what I believed was meant to be was going to be. My emotions got in the backseat and I was all business.

I remember the doctor who came to console me after the neurologist said he was dying. She kneeled down and was rubbing my arm. I looked at her emotionless and asked, "Is he alive?" When she confirmed that he was, I said, "I want him transferred then." It didn't matter what she said after that, I didn't care who she was or what degree she had. That was MY child, and I'm making the decisions. You get my kid out of here! I spent the rest of Corbin's recovery like that. I knew in my heart what his outcome was going to be, and I wasn't willing to let anything get in my way.

I never sat in his room, even on that first night when I knew we could lose him at any minute, and pictured how life would be without him. What his empty seat at Thanksgiving would look like. What Christmas morning would feel like without his bear hugs as he opened his favorite gift, or how I would handle Grace going to her first prom and not having Corbin there in the picture for his senior prom. I never imagined if I could handle attending his graduation knowing his name wouldn't be called but only spoken in memory.

I couldn't do that. I wouldn't allow my mind to go there or I wouldn't have had the strength to fight for him like I did. But . . . once he was home, it hit me.

On Thanksgiving, it was the kids and I, including Mari getting ready. I was in the kitchen cooking, and Mari and Grace turned the music up and started a dance party around the kitchen. Corbin was still scared to stand for too long due to the passing out, so they pulled a chair up for him. The girls danced around the island and he danced in his seat and it hit, what if he wasn't here? He almost wasn't and I started crying. I was so thankful.

I couldn't even imagine my existence without him. The same thing happened at Christmas and New Year's. He was my hero and no matter what else was falling apart around me, having him was all that mattered.

Corbin started tutoring at home slowly and gradually worked

up to five days a week back at school for two hours a day. For someone with a brain injury, everything is exhausting so between his new tutoring schedule and six therapy appointments a week it started to take its toll on Corbin. I started noticing his memory declining and I approached therapy and the school, and we cut everything back.

The number one goal was always to let Corbin heal and it was backfiring. He had been making huge progress in all his therapies, and most of them agreed he needed a break. This was about the same time as prom, and six months since Corbin came home.

Grace hadn't had the easiest return to school that year. Corbin's accident had made her realize what was really important in life much sooner than her friends. She found she couldn't relate to her friends who were the same age anymore and who were still caught up in high school drama. The accident pushed her maturity into fast forward.

Despite Grace having a somewhat long-term boyfriend for that age, when it was time for prom she wanted to go with Corbin. She came to me at first and asked if I thought that was weird and of course I didn't. I thought it was the best idea ever! I hadn't let Corbin out of my sight. If I was going to, at least it would be with Grace. She protected him like I did, and that became the plan.

We shopped for the perfect dress, and we got Corbin a navy suit he picked out. Grace, my Pinterest queen, found the perfect flowers for them. We ordered and we pulled it all off. Pictures were taken, and Corbin, Grace, and Tanna left to pick up Tanna's girlfriend.

The rest of us left for the local function center where the prom was being held. Every year they do a prom "lineup." All of the couples or friends going together line up as their names are called, and they make their walk down the long sidewalk lined with family and friends eager to take pictures. We got their early to get a perfect picture spot, but I started to stress as I hadn't seen the car pull in with them yet.

I texted Grace, who assured me they were close. As soon as they got there, they jumped in line and she assured me they were there and okay. I was definitely having a bit of separation anxiety. Granted, it had been months since he had arrived home, but he had only been out of my sight three times with Dad, and a few others with my mother, or with Paul who had brought him to therapy here and there. Now, he was with other teenagers driving him, and it was like cutting the umbilical cord all over again. I took a deep breath knowing they were there.

As we stood there, I jointly kept an eye out for them in the line and chasing Grayson, who was all too bored with this standing around. When I saw them in line, third to be called, I broke down. I turned around and put my hands over my face and sobbed. A few seconds later, my mother saw and asked what was wrong. I said, "He's here."

She giggled a little, and said, "Were you that worried they weren't going to make it in time?"

I cried harder and said, "No, he's actually here! He was so close to missing this, us missing this. He's actually at his senior prom."

Those are the times it all hit me. Christmas, prom, walking at his graduation, that's when the what-ifs, picturing him not being there hit me, and they still do. From seeing him sit with Grayson and making him laugh, jumping in the pool, playing video games with Corbin, or listening to his name being called to walk up at graduation. Nothing is taken for granted. You make these bargains with beings or people, or whoever might be listening. Then, when they're granted, for whatever reason, you are grateful for every minute you have after that.

Last Monday was the trial for the driver, and I knew we were going to be hounded by the media. So, I took the kids to Portsmouth. We walked by the water and stopped in Prescott Park. Corbin, Cohen, and Grayson were playing tag. I sat there in amazement watching him run around with his brothers. It's hard to not picture how bad he was when you see things like that.

As I write this, Corbin's accident was one year and eight months ago. We have been to Boston for follow-ups countless times, hundreds of therapy appointments, and year-round tutoring. We have laughed, and we have cried. But in the end, we are good. Life is good. It's not the same and it never will be.

Corbin could live with me for the next three years, or he could live with me for the rest of his life, and either option would be fine. We still live in the unknown, to an extent, because a brain injury takes many years but that's okay. I would take our worst day over the alternative every second of my life.

THANK YOU

I really need to take this opportunity to thank so many people. I didn't get through this by myself. I didn't become the person or mother I am without so many people by my side.

My mother started it all. She was the best mother a person could ever be blessed with. I grew up knowing that I was always wanted and loved. She has been my mother, my friend, and my biggest supporter, my whole life. Her love for me gave me my biggest desire to have children of my own. She is a second mother to my children, and she loves them as much as me.

She was at the hospital before me the day of Corbin's accident and never left my side unless she was taking care of my other kids or she was forced. She is the reason the kids and I still have a roof over our heads. She taught me the strength that I needed to get through the most difficult time of my life and keep fighting every day afterward. She is who I look up to and have always aspired to be like. Thank you, Mom, for being my rock.

My kids next. Poor Grayson had his life uprooted at just two years old. Mostly everyone and everything in his daily life changed. Cohen was the same. He spent most of his school vacation in the hospital. He lived with dad half the time and Gramma the other half. No familiar bedroom or usual toys, no visits with friends. He watched his big brother fight for his life, and he remained strong and positive the whole time.

And then my Grace. She was with me day in and day out. She stood by Corbin's side and mine. She gave up friends and her whole social life to support her family and she came out even stronger. She remains an honor student in the national honor society. Grace is even graduating, a year early, at the age of sixteen to pursue a career in medicine, inspired by her brother's journey. She is the most incredible, thoughtful, caring, hardworking, loving child a parent could only imagine having. I love you all, and I'm so proud and grateful I get to call you all mine!

Paul Raymond you are next. I have no doubt in my mind that Corbin wouldn't be alive if it wasn't for you. By some miracle you were one of the first people at the hospital and guided me the rest of the way. You always kept this calm, cool attitude, you knew the questions to ask and what to do next. You were by our side the whole way, from visiting, to running the kids back and forth, to getting Corbin anything he needed, to staying with him when no one else could, to fundraising. You were incredible, and I will forever be thankful for all you have done for us!

Jenn Childs, you have been my longest, dearest friend. You jumped into action doing anything and everything you could, immediately. The countless trips back and forth to Boston, taking care of my home and animals, my bills, organizing fundraisers and working at them, to even finding a great new home for our dog when we knew we weren't coming home anytime soon. You did it all without ever being asked, and I love you.

Jan Raymond, you were always my favorite. As difficult as this time was you were one of the best things that came from it. Your support and love mean the world to me. You are another example of the kind of mom only certain lucky children get to grow up with and moms like me learn how to be better from. Thank you for being a part of our lives.

Auntie (Christine Cushing) you are my other blessing that came from all of this. You love my kids like they're your own. All of your support, tears, and laughs throughout all of this and that continues today. You're selfless, always thinking of others like helping Corbin give back to Spaulding with the toy drive you organize. We're so lucky to have you in our lives.

Tanna Valliere you are one remarkable kid. Your bravery is the reason Corbin is still here today. You had just been through the most terrifying event of your life and as that mangled car with a crushed roof finally rested on its side against the tree, you didn't try to save your own life and get out. You thought of Corbin. You stayed in that car with all of its uncertainties and kept your best friend alive. That says so much about who you are, Tanna, a real-life hero. We all love you so much.

Rosa our favorite nurse. Thank you for not just treating Corbin but caring for him like he was yours. We got so lucky the first day you walked into that room. You not only became my friend, but you also became family to us. We will always be thankful for everything you have done.

Brenda Baron, you did so much for the kids and me. So much more than you had to, or I would have ever asked you to do. All the times you brought Grayson to see me, taking care of Grayson, the messages asking what I needed, telling me what a good job I was doing, the fundraising, and then the house. You got volunteers and busted your tail to transform our house so we would have a beautiful, comfortable home to return to. You're amazing and I'm so grateful to call you family.

Todd Civin, thank you for believing in our story and taking on this role to help share it with the world. Thank you for being patient when I needed it and also giving me a little kick when I needed that. None of this would be possible without you.

I wish that I had all of the names of the nurses, doctors, fire, rescue, helicopter pilots, and anyone else who worked on Corbin. You are all my heroes. You all took part in saving Corbin's life. He wouldn't be here without you, and I will forever be grateful for you.

Corbin you have challenged me from the start. First ambulance ride, first stitches, life-threatening allergy scares, and then this. Mom's heart can't take much more so it's time to stop but, in all seriousness, you are my miracle. Your determination and positive attitude inspire me every day. Thank you for being that kid, for fighting. I'm so proud of who you are, how far you've come, and I can't wait to see all the possibilities the future hold for you. I love you with every fiber in my body buddy.

Last but not least, I need to thank every single other person who sent a message, cooked meals for us, bought a bracelet, said a prayer, wished us well, came to visit, volunteered, mowed our lawn, plowed our driveway, the list is endless. The love and support we were given is mind-blowing; kindness matters.

I had a nurse at Spaulding tell me that the support Corbin had is why he made this kind of recovery. She said that she had been doing the job for years, and yes, of course the medical part of it plays a huge role. But beyond being alive, Corbin thrived. Having his family by his side, showing him the love and support is what gives people the will to fight and keep pushing. I believe in the power of love and positivity.

So many people have told me they wouldn't have been able to do the things I've done, but I don't believe that. I believe we all have an inner strength that we know nothing about until we're put to this kind of test. We have to keep positivity even when there seems to be nothing to be positive about. Find the smallest thing and hold onto it. For me, it was the fact that Corbin was alive. As long as he was still alive, I wasn't giving up.

Everyone one of you gave me that inner strength to keep fighting, and I thank you all!

We would like to take a moment to thank the merchants in our local area who participated in our Kickstarter campaign enabling us to raise the funds needed to publish our book *121 Days*. Without their help and support, this project would not have been possible.

Merchant Sponsor Double Platinum
Cheney's Apple House Furniture
Penacook, NH 03303
Escape Room
Concord, NH 03301
Smoke Shack Southern Barbecue
Boscawen, NH 03303
4 McNeil Enterprise LLC
Loudon, NH 03307

Merchant Sponsor Platinum
Franklin Savings Bank
Boscawen, NH 03303
Granite Hill Municipal Services
Concord, NH 03301

Merchant Sponsor Gold

Active Choice Healthcare
Concord, NH 03301
The Dumpster Depot
Canterbury, NH 03224
Huckleberry Propane and Oil LLC
Boscawen, NH 03303
Taylored Image
Strafford, NH 03884

Merchant Sponsor Supporter

Homestead Inn
Boscawen, NH 03303
Love for Lexi
Penacook, NH 03303